Afoot
in Connecticut

Journeys in Natural History

Afoot
in Connecticut

Journeys in Natural History

Eric D. Lehman

HOMEBOUND
PUBLICATIONS
Independent Publisher of Contemplative Titles

PUBLISHED BY HOMEBOUND PUBLICATIONS

For bulk ordering information or permissions write:
Homebound Publications, PO Box 1442
Pawcatuck, Connecticut 06379 United States of America

Visit us at: www.homeboundpublications.com

FIRST EDITION
ISBN: 978-1-938846-07-6 (pbk)

BOOK DESIGN
Front Cover Image: © Eric D. Lehman
Back Cover Image: Macedonia Brook State Park, Connecticut
Back Cover Image Attribution: © Spirit of America (shuttershock.com)
Cover and Interior Design: Leslie M. Browning

Library of Congress Cataloging-in-Publication Data

Lehman, Eric D.
  Afoot in Connecticut : journeys in natural history / Eric D. Lehman. —First edition.
    pages cm
  Includes bibliographical references.
  ISBN 978-1-938846-07-6 (paperback)
  1. Natural history—Connecticut. 2. Lehman, Eric D.—Travel—Connecticut. 3. Connecticut—Description and travel. 4. Connecticut—History, Local. I. Title.
  QH105.C8L44 2013
  508.746--dc23

                                                                                2012051550

10 9 8 7 6 5 4 3 2 1

ALSO BY ERIC D. LEHMAN

Insiders' Guide to Connecticut

Bridgeport: Tales From the Park City

Hamden: Tales from the Sleeping Giant

*Becoming Tom Thumb: Charles Stratton, P.T. Barnum,
and the Dawn of American Celebrity*

CO-AUTHOR WITH AMY NAWROCKI

A History of Connecticut Food

A History of Connecticut Wine

Table
of Contents

Afoot and in the open road,
one has a fair start in life at last.
— JOHN BURROUGHS, *The Exhilarations of the Road*

Chapter One

A Land of Sleeping Giants

On a quiet summer day I parked under the white pines at Sleeping Giant State Park and shouldered a heavy pack full of love letters. Heading down the rocky path, I paused at the Mill River, watched a fisherman cast for trout, and then headed up the trail to the old quarry. A happy couple frolicked below on the grassy meadow, and I looked away, gripping my walking stick up the steep, barren ridge, past a twisted tree, up and up into the sky. Breathing heavily, crushed under the weight of the load, I struggled my way up the edge of the quarry, and beyond it to the flat forehead of the Giant, where I rested on a large boulder.

Instead of continuing on the trail to the cliffs that formed the monstrous chin, I turned left into the sparse forest and yellow grasses, heading down again past the falcon nests, carefully placing feet on the steep, pathless slope. Finally, in a small vertical meadow I set the pack down and tested the earth with my walking stick. Finding an appropriate spot, I took out my small primus stove and boiled water, letting the wind blow my hair from my face. When the brew had finished, I sipped the steaming tea, idly sifting through the box of letters, reading a line here and there. Then, putting the empty mug away, I pulled a shovel from the heavy pack and began to dig.

When I first moved to Connecticut, my explorations of the Nutmeg state began with my car. I drove through nearly every town, on every road, following the gray lines of my topographic maps. I found villages and lakes that existed in no guide book. I traveled on weekends and weekdays, stopping for coffee at diners and for pizza at delis. I put forty thousand miles on my car in this way. Much of that time I was driving to trailheads, or searching for them, because the best way to know a country is on foot. All the great explorers and writers will tell you this. And so, I took them literally, and began to give up my car in favor of my own two legs. I wanted to explore every inch of path in the state that had become my home.

Connecticut is often the most overlooked of the New England states. Other states have higher mountains, grander beaches, more famous cities. Other states in the area have become famous, while we seem to linger in relative obscurity, caught between the city-pinchers of Boston and New York. But it is that very obscurity which leaves our state so precious for the walker. Instead of giant parks or famous resorts, we have quiet country lanes and villages. We also have more walking space per acre than many other states. Where I grew up, southeast Pennsylvania, trails are few and far between. There are a few long greenways, but no real trail networks and a scattering of state parks, spread out over an area the size of our own modest state. Here there seemed to be endless possibilities. I steadily checked off each walk in the various hiking guides. I clocked miles on the Blue Trail system, paging through the famed Connecticut Walk Book. And with my Atlas of Connecticut Topographical Maps, I found other paths and trails, old roads that led nowhere, and hidden hills that no trail led to.

All this time I was creating memories—Letting tired feet dangle in the lovely cascade at Southford Falls. Running on the boardwalk above the swamp at Dinosaur State Park, the state's premier paleontological site. Watching the crashing winter Sound through the frame of the railroad tunnel at Rocky Neck. Writing a poem while perching on a stream-boulder in Twin Brooks Park in Trumbull and reading Stephen Graham's The Gentle Art of Tramping on a cool bed of damp moss by the Natchaug River. Smelling the salt air while watching white sailboats and gray fishing boats from the old lighthouse at Stonington Point. And lying in a high meadow of long grass on the ridge of Osborndale State Park, at one with the magnificent, cloud-blue sky.

Though I have lived in Connecticut for less than two decades, I have hiked so often that the memories blur and darken already. I know that the first wild place I walked was Sleeping Giant, and I vaguely remember the first time I visited, reading the tangled trail map and ambitiously decided on a circumnavigation of the park. But I remember absolutely nothing of the actual hike. It has been overwritten by dozens of other rambles over the Giant's limbs. All told, I have wandered here over a hundred times, with dozens of friends and students, all of them overlapping in memory like crowds of ghosts.

But those hikes were still in the future that summer day when I perched on the empty side of the Giant's head, burying a box of love letters in the rocky earth. Those letters, or the woman who sent them to me, were the only reason I had come to Connecticut, and now she had left me. Multi-colored letters declaring love and longing had no place in a world without her, or indeed without any human presence. But I couldn't quite bring myself to throw them away. I wanted to let them dissolve there, to give the earthworms some good roughage. Perhaps I was littering, I don't know. At any rate, I finished digging, and placed the box deep in the earth. Dirt and rocks followed. Then I stood quietly there on that seldom-seen spot, down the steep tilting slope between the cliffs.

Barely a minute passed before a doe and newborn fawn stepped carefully by, not twenty yards away. I stood absolutely still and they looked directly at me and either did not see or did not care. The mother and child seemed to bless my enterprise, and as I buried my past, I felt the newness and awkwardness of my next life beginning, a walking life on the brownstone paths of Connecticut. But on that day I had no clue how extraordinary my journeys would become: that I would explore hidden caves, track countless wild animals, and attempt hikes clear across the state. I had no idea how this land of gentle mountains and little rivers would change me.

But I could see the first step ahead. Shading my eyes and turning north, I could see across the state, to a hundred other special places like this one, and then the map of our entire state was before my eyes, blue trails and greenways spread out like the arteries of a larger giant, one that only waits for us to wake it with the tapping of a thousand tiny walking sticks. My pack was light as I walked away from the tomb of love letters. It was a fine place to start again.

Chapter Two

Walking the Shore

My first memories of Connecticut are of the shady back streets of West Haven. My college girlfriend and I moved from Pennsylvania to an apartment on Elm Street, on which there were no elms. And so, the first thing I learned about my new home was what was missing, these gorgeous, ancient trees that had once lined the streets of America. They had been gone for decades, but like a fading romance, the memory lingered.

The elms that lent their name to our street began to disappear in 1928. Brought in on imported furniture timber, Dutch Elm disease swept through southwest Connecticut quickly, killing many of the venerable trees in under a decade, and the remaining ones in the next few decades. Spread by the elm bark beetle, the sickness was discovered by a Dutch scientist, giving it a slightly misleading name. The upper branches of the vase-shaped trees began to turn yellow long before autumn, and they die and fall off, with the disease progressing down the tree. The roots starved without the nutrients brought from the leaves, and the huge trunks had to be chopped down before they fell and crushed the houses crouched fearfully beneath them.

A few years after colonization, the "Elm City" of New Haven initiated the first public tree planting program in America, and elms had flourished there. In Wethersfield, the largest and tallest elm in the country survived from 1758, growing to ninety-seven feet fall, thirty feet around, with a hundred and forty seven foot spread. It was called "the most magnificent tree east of the Rockies," but it was helpless against the disease, which finally killed it in 1953. Many of the other trees, weakened by the disease, fell in the hurricane of 1938.

Trying to ignore this absence, we left Elm Street and rambled through the town, taking various routes to the beach. Dogs barked in the overgrown yards of the clapboard beach-town houses, run down and converted into year-round residences. Unseen birds hid in vacant lots, singing cautious songs. Reaching Long Island Sound, we walked along the seaside path from New Haven harbor to Milford, picking up shells and peering across the summer waters. Absences followed us, though, like the missing Savin Rock Amusement Park, once the "Coney Island of Connecticut," now a tangle of twisted metal at the bottom of the Sound. Above the drowned roller coasters, the splashing waters mingled with the cries of the gulls, filling our hearts with strange, antique longings. Other travelers passed us, some with dogs, or babies, or elderly relatives. Some ran, or biked, or rollerbladed. But a few just walked on this natural border, gazing away from the sprawling town, towards the cobalt sea.

This was my first exposure to the budding walking culture I had first encountered at college in Ohio, where an old railway had been transformed into a bike path, linking my small, isolated campus with the nearby town. The same girlfriend I would move to Connecticut with wandered with me in ever-increasing spirals from our hoary, ivy-clothed rooms. We had no plan, simply feeling our way through pungent farms and under flowering hedges. We passed crumbling churches, quaint homesteads, and rippling streams. And we discovered that we were not the only ones walking. In middle America, a reaction against the car-driven suburban culture had begun. Was this an old-world, European reaction to our fast-paced modern society? Or was this something very new? I didn't know, but I was glad to be a part of it.

Here in Connecticut I encountered this culture again. I would find repurposed canals and railways, called greenways, similar to the one I had tramped in Ohio, springing up across our state. An extensive blue-trail system added a wild element that would thrill me even more. I hadn't found any of these yet, though, and stayed by the ocean, tracing a nautical map with my feet. I would stop at Sherwood Island or Silver Sands State Park in the afternoons between classes, wandering the winding paths by the salt marshes, searching for elusive mammals under copses of trees, and examining crustaceans along the rim of the beach. I watched children flying kites at Harkness Memorial Park, lying on the grassy slope that led down to the ever-present sea.

I nostalgically associated the sea and the sandy beach in particular with childhood summer weeks on the Jersey shore and, unfortunately for me, with vacations to Cape Hatteras and Cape Cod with this college girlfriend, whom we'll call Ingrid. She was sweet and tried her best to make things work in our new apartment home. I was distant and cold with her, not ready for commitment, attached to the so-called freedoms of my youth and to the large groups of friends I'd left behind. After less than a year together in West Haven, she broke up with me, and for good reason. I was left alone in this strange place, away from old friends and family. I considered moving back to Pennsylvania, but then teaching opportunities kept me here, and I knew my destiny was intertwined with Connecticut's.

I had spent the last ten years of my life amidst friends, surrounded by the warmth and chaos of high school, college, and graduate school. And I had given all that up to follow her here, where she was attending graduate school, to become a colony of two rather than two dozen. I didn't know what to do with all this space. So, sometimes I would nap like a tramp on the picnic tables or hide like a hermit in the pine groves. Occasionally I would attempt a vertical walk, climbing one of the few elder trees that overhung the fens. Anything to make these experiences different, more important and special.

The easiest place to do this was at Hammonasset State Park. Named for the local Indian tribe, this gem is probably the only long stretch of pristine beach to walk in the state. One autumn day I spent a full ten hours at Hammonasset with Ingrid walking the long length of the seafront, then relaxing and watching the gulls and kites play in the gray sky, and finally forging into the marshy back paths, where we listened to various and distinct birdsongs. Purple martins and herons flapped through the muddy salt flats and the bayberry thickets on small islands. Sanderlings skittered along the beach, pecking for insects and clams.

Upon leaving I remarked on the perfect day, and Ingrid noted that we had not ventured into the water itself. Well, I was no swimmer. I had found my own secret joy. I wanted to keep walking, to head down the beach, perhaps to walk all the way home parallel to Route One's long expanse, that ancient Pequot War Path turned stoplight nightmare. Alfred Milford Turner, a schoolteacher from Litchfield, had done this very thing in 1914 when he was commissioned to find the best places for our shoreline parks. Turner was dedicated to the conservation of Connecticut's lands, and a temporary appointment from the state became a twenty-eight year life work. He said, "I found the shore of Long Island Sound an almost endless row of individual vagaries, nondescript caricatures of habitation, alternating with miles of sea-walls, land-walls, and hedges, behind which towered huge piles of granite, brick, or concrete, which I judged also to be habitations, though the casual democratic eye might frequently conclude otherwise. I tried to imagine the changes of the next thirty years, and still future thirties, and very gradually I began to perceive that natural scenic beauty and the unrestricted private ownership of land are things apart, and quite incompatible."[1]

Today, despite the work of Turner and others, large stretches of private lands and restricted beaches unfortunately makes walking them for any length difficult. So, although Hammonasset has the longest beach, Rocky Neck State Park was my favorite for a long time, but not for its charming half-moon bay. No, because I could park two miles away and walk. I realize that this is not a big selling point for most sun-worshippers. Nevertheless, I usually parked in a turnout along the winding road between Old Lyme and Niantic. The woodland trail immediately opened into a large meadow, where once I watched two deer teach a fawn to browse. The trail wound along the salt marsh, back into the forest, and along a ridge overlooking the silent railroad tracks. Then, after crossing the rails, the trail reached a pavilion above the beach. Reaching a golden strip of burning sand this way made the inevitable relaxation that much sweeter. I always felt like I'd earned my lazy, easy beach-time.

Formed by the ancient Laurentian Ice Sheet, our beaches have seen many changes since the first humans reached this shore, probably journeying from the northwest, ten thousand years ago. The scooped-out sea must have seemed like a banquet to those who had known the cold swamps and fir-trees that huddled by the retreating glaciers. When the pilgrims landed the coasts were tree-dotted parkland, fire-managed by the natives, populated by the heath hen. Huge feasts of clams and oysters took place throughout those epochs, the beaches providing a wonderful freedom during the festive summer months. But with the arrival of Europeans, slow changes over eons became swift changes over mere decades.

The larger fauna we destroyed immediately: mountain lions, bears, and wolves were hunted as pests, and deer and moose for food. The birds took longer, and generally proved harder to kill. However, a few proved too easy. The heath hen, a subspecies of the greater prairie chicken, lived in the large park-like areas created by Native Americans and natural heaths near the Connecticut coast. There were so many in the 1700s that only the poor ate them, but by the middle of the 1800s they were extinct on the Connecticut mainland. They lingered on the islands, with the last dying on Martha's Vineyard in 1932, despite efforts to save them.

Unlike the more reclusive heath hen, the passenger pigeon blacked out the sky in vast migratory waves. Billions lived in America before Europeans arrived, and they remained in large numbers until the 1800s, when they became a cheap food to feed to slaves and the immigrant poor. Hunting on a scale nearly unbelievable today took place, with each hunter using the more accurate new guns to shoot hundreds of birds from the sky each day. The pigeons bred in large social groups, and no one realized that reducing their population so quickly caused an even sharper decline. Connecticut was part of their breeding zone, and increased development into their nesting areas contributed to the disaster. The number of survivors was too few, and the passenger pigeons vanished forever.

The seascape had changed, too. When Europeans arrived in the New World, they found lobsters five feet long living in the Sound, and speedily devoured them all. The oysters that the natives had feasted on were also huge and numerous, living in banks the size of coral reefs. These tasty bivalves were huge, and immediately became a delicacy in Europe. Connecticut oystermen harvested them by the boatload. By the 1800s the natural oysters were gone, but aquaculture farming replaced them, for a while. Then pollution brought on parasites that wiped out 90% of the oyster beds in the 1990s. And now, much of the bottom of the Sound looks like a desert, devoid of the nitrogen-filtering power of oysters.

You wouldn't know that just looking at the wine-dark water from the beautiful beaches along Connecticut's gentle shore, or rather the tiny percentage of our beaches that has been set off for public use. There is just enough space for everyone to place a blanket, lie back, and watch the cloudless sky. As Alfred Turner found nearly a century ago, for a serious walker these spaces are quickly insufficient. But I was not one of those yet and loved every step taken in these precious natural enclaves.

Milford Point Bird Sanctuary is one of these rare gems, pitifully small for a nature refuge, hemmed in by houses, watched carefully by the city across the Housatonic River. Despite this, or perhaps because of it, Milford Point served as my oracle one crisp September day. The sanctuary hid piping plovers and least tern nests among the scanty dunes. Yellow marsh grass protected strange black-headed ducks. I wandered out onto a curving spit of sand, covered by millions of red and white shells. The lagoon created by low tide, peppered with tufts of marsh grass, was a dwarf version of the large salt marsh tucked behind the spear-like point itself. These intertidal zones, with their briny smell and vital filtering properties provide some of the most important habitat in the state. Hundreds of migrating birds, aquatic animals, and land animals use these wonderful, nutrient-rich areas. The crabs, clams, and steamers that live in the mud flats feed on the smaller fauna and flora, and feed both humans and birds. But this was no longer a place for us to gather the few that remained.

Once, the largest salt marsh in what today is Connecticut was formed a little farther east by the Quinnipiac and Mill Rivers. The city of New Haven had been founded in the midst of this marsh, primarily for defensive purposes. But then as populations grew, that salt marsh and others across the jagged coastline were filled in, dredged, and drained. This practice was slowed down in 1969 with the Tidal Wetland Act, though what remained of our relatively quiet coastal marshes continued to degrade.

One area that outwardly remains is Barn Island, right on the border with Rhode Island, a great place to watch for birds quietly and slowly. Over a thousand acres are protected, the largest coastal property in the state managed for wildlife conservation. Small hills, open fields, and small forests spread out into coffee-colored tidal wetlands. However, even this was diked after World War II, causing it to become a freshwater marsh in the mid-20th century. Work has been done in the last few decades to reverse this, eliminating invasive species and restoring it to its original state as a tidal marsh. But thousands of acres along the Connecticut coast are not salvageable, and more disappears every day.

Two girls flew a rainbow kite on the grasses near the shore houses that surrounded the tiny beach at Milford Point. About twelve houses perched on the end of the point beyond the nature center with its observation tower. No doubt these homes were very expensive, and they didn't seem to interfere with the birds. However, they did hinder human observers like myself. Charles Island was barely visible to the east, the place where Captain Kidd's treasure was reputed to be buried. Small planes landed at the local airport on the west side of the river. Gulls bobbed on the deep blue water. Wind blew waves from inland onto this thin spit of sand, driftwood, and gravel. I had sat with Ingrid on the strand of low shell beach just a few months earlier. The overlapping waves creating fascinating geometric patterns, as they had done that spring day. Now, the first hints of death touched the leaves of the small, struggling chestnuts at the nature center.

Like the elms, chestnut trees have mostly departed from the state. When the first European settlers arrived in Connecticut, the forests were primarily white pine and chestnuts. These were cut down for ships masts and lumber, but many chestnuts remained until a terrible airborne fungal blight swept through in the early 20th century. It was first noticed in the Bronx Zoo in 1904, and spread fifty miles annually, killing Connecticut's mature trees in a few deadly years. The blasted shells of these massive hardwood trees occasionally linger in the state's forests, but few live ones remain other than scattered, small hybrids.

I climbed the winding stair to the Audubon Observation Tower and gazed over the myriad yellow-green islands of marsh grass in the lagoon. Herons picked through the mudflats, framed by smoke stacks on the horizon. Speedboats and sailboats swayed offshore, while more waited at the myriad docks for their human masters. As the sun dropped over Stratford, I felt once again that closed-in, overpopulated sensation. We are too many and nature has become the precious ruby in our midst.

Extinctions and reductions surrounded me that day. Ingrid and I had separated, and now I was without friends, without love, and without a clue what to do next. And yet, somehow things did not look so bleak. Why? Was it the slanting sunlight sparkling on the Housatonic River? Perhaps. Or perhaps I knew that extinction can be a chance for something else to grow. Scientists have now developed new Elms and Chestnuts resistant to disease, and some have been planted in Connecticut. The mountain lions are still gone, but bears and moose have returned. Coyotes live here now instead of wolves. The oysters would return. And the birds! More than three hundred bird species regularly visit Connecticut, and one hundred and seventy five nest here. That was a lot yet to see, to understand, and to work to preserve.

I looked upriver, to the promising forests and rocky hills. Perhaps that could be the place to make a solitary future, without romance or companionship. I could hike new paths, find new hope, and fall in love with the natural wonders that still flourished here. I could seek the new, the transitory, the rare. Beaches would always be a part of me, but they were too narrow to walk forever.

Chapter Three

Within the Magic Grove

When I continued exploring Connecticut, I thought I needed purpose, some activity to justify my travels. I started by taking books to read with me into the woods. One day at Sleeping Giant, I hiked alone at my own brisk pace, stepping quietly through the lush woods with my long legs, rambling along the trails, crossing ancient stone property boundaries, using segments of four old logging tote roads. I clambered up a rocky slope, across a sunlit meadow, and found a hidden tarn in a deep hollow. I sat on a nearby clifflet and ate lunch, reading Robert Louis Stevenson's *Travels With A Donkey*. I quickly found out my site was near to Hezekiah's Knob and the popular white-blazed trail as several groups of walkers passed me by, though none noticed me, dressed in gray and green, motionless upon the outstretched finger of rock. It was a great place to read a book, but somehow that wasn't all I was looking for.

Sometimes I took field guides with me, identifying animals in the pursuit of knowledge for its own sake. Once I scared a wild turkey, who ran through the brush for about twenty yards, then took off into the air with a great flapping of wings and circled around behind me. I saw blue jays, chipmunks, and a box turtle which I moved off the trail onto a warm rock, afraid a careless biker or dog would hurt him. Red-headed wood-peckers pattered on dead snags and banded chipmunks chattered under the leaves. When animals were not enough, I turned to trees and plants, checking species off a long list, pleased with my progress.

A charming hobbit-like couple foraging for edible mushrooms en-gaged me in conversation on one occasion, and I mentioned several other places around the state I had recently seen these treats. I had never tried mushrooming, but thought about it many times. I found dozens of so-cieties and clubs devoted to this pastime, something I would discover was not unusual for any outdoor activity pursued in our woodlands. In this case, hundreds of amateur mycologists hunted edges of streams and shady bowers, collecting, identifying, and at last eating mushrooms. A mushroomer could be recognized by a basket, a pocket knife, a magnify-ing lens, and a field guide tucked into a front pocket. These field guides are indispensable, since there is no rule that distinguishes edible and poi-sonous mushrooms. Even experts often mistake a deadly species for a delicious treat. This danger only provides a bit of spice to this pursuit, I'm sure, but it may have been the factor that kept me from its subtle joys and rewards.

Leaving the two mushroomers, I wandered through a hopeful chestnut plantation, crushing the spiny shells underfoot, and waved to a strange birder who was filming something unseen in a tree. I thought about becoming a more meticulous birder, having seen and listened to dozens if not hundreds of species of birds while here in Connecticut. My favorites are the red-tailed hawks, which seem omnipresent, hovering over me as I hike, waiting for some sign of weakness, perhaps hoping that the machinery of my legs will rust or snap. These muscular, agile birds hunt along the edges of forests, using tall trees as lookouts, waiting and watching for their moment to strike a passing mouse or squirrel. Once they were hunted without mercy by the farmers of our state, but now they thrive once again, yelling their fearsome "keeeer-r-r" across the sky.

In those early years I'd seen a fantastic green bird while hiking in Hubbard Park in Meriden. Green? I puzzled over this oddity for a long time, until I saw more, swooping around Seaside Park in Bridgeport. They wheeled past classrooms, challenged the monolith of the University library, and settled on the statue of P.T. Barnum. The mystery of these emerald birds confused me as I taught my way through the literary canon. There are no green birds in New England, I told myself stubbornly. Then again, my classes were filled with international students from over eighty countries, so why not these avian invaders from thirty degrees latitude further south?

The mystery's solution was not easy to divine. I was told by field guides that these were simply house pet escapees from the urban wastelands of the northeast, gathering together in groups, much the same way my students sometimes separated by nationality in the cafeteria. One local told me that a truck had overturned on I-95 and released them all at once. The only sure information was that numerous pockets of these out-of-place creatures existed throughout the New York metropolitan area. They had no problem surviving the cold New England winters, and live a long time, adapting and thriving. This was a breeding population, not some freak group that froze to death when times got hard. I see them every spring, greeting me as I return from break, no doubt here to stay.

But I did not have the painstaking patience for birding, nor the gambling spirit of a mushroomer. Then, on a hike to Ragged Mountain between Meriden and Hartford I found another activity that tempted me. Ragged Mountain is really only a series of escarpments, barely a hill. I planned to make the entire loop, but cut it off halfway. And it was lucky I did. Sometimes a wander off the prescribed path brings adventure and discovery. This time I discovered several wonderfully rusting cars that had been here for at least forty or fifty years growing into the brush. One had a flowering bush blooming from its hood. I wished briefly I was a car expert, so I could identify the models and years. But they looked old, certainly. I also clambered on the so-called "Chinese wall," a natural formation that seemed to be a wall made by giants. Of course, what appeared to be joined two-ton blocks really was one massive rock, cracked by the centuries of elements. Regardless, it inspired legends and fables, which is sometimes more important.

The view from these hills was vast: of the backside of the Hanging Hills in Meriden, of the Litchfield Hills to the west, of Talcott Mountain to the north. And it overlooked several reservoirs, cobalt blue against the sea of green trees. This baffled me at the time—I was near the center of suburban Connecticut, of sprawling civilization, but could see very little evidence. No matter which direction my brown eyes strayed from the elliptical route, the ubiquitous trees buried every human signpost. Then I stumbled into rock climbers scaling the cliffs on the south side of Ragged Mountain, peering down their rainbow of ropes and waving. I watched these climbers for awhile, thinking that they had these views all the time, and then continued along the orange ledges to the reservoir.

Over the next few months I researched this activity finding that Connecticut has a surprising number of short climbs, though of course no truly big walls. Most of it is bolt climbing or top-rope. At Chatfield Hollow, I talked with some climbers shooting bolts into a cliff, the metal-on-stone sound reverberating in the rocky hollows. Another time I met a man at the same place who was clearly removing them, engaged in an intracultural battle of wills and methods. This rock-climbing subculture was even more tempting than the birders or mushroomers, but I never took the final step to join.

I toyed with the idea of mountain biking at the mysterious West-woods Preserve and Park, a place with a huge network of trails, similar to Sleeping Giant without the vertical extremes. Still, there are plenty of cliffs and caves to explore, if you can handle the occasional off-road cyclist screaming down the paths. Then one day I found another problem. The large rocky shelf at the southwest corner of Westwoods, overlooking a deep forested valley, was literally caked in shards of broken bottle-glass. I shuddered to think of what a fall would do to a mountain biker here. The unavoidable glass crunched ominously beneath my boots. The open, smooth rock that created great biking had also made this a great area for illegal campfires by rowdy partiers. I could see the attraction of that, too, I supposed, though not the carelessness with glass. I didn't want to be careless, or to go through the forests at speed. I wanted to sit on a windy ledge and stare across a salty lake at a pine-stream island, and to think.

The day I discovered what carelessness had done to that beautiful spot, I had another encounter. A large dog ran up to me, panting. I knelt down and petted him, then looked up as the owner approached. My breath caught. A gorgeous blonde girl with sunglasses stood in front of me.

"Do you know which way to Dunk Hill Road?" she asked, smiling.

"Yeah, I've got a map." I fumbled with my equipment.

"Well, that's smart." The girl and her big dog leapt up the slope along-side me. She moved with ease, and I suddenly felt slow and cumbersome.

I retrieved the map and pointed out her route. "You've got the right trail; you're just going the wrong way."

"Yeah, I was following Spike. I went over around the loop, but I wasn't sure how to go back this way."

We talked about where we hiked in Connecticut. I stared admiringly at her angular jawline and graceful hands. Her curve around shades hid her eyes, but her short yellow hair fell fetchingly around her face.

"Well, nice to meet you...oh, I'm Eric."

"Tara. Nice to meet you." We shook hands, laughing.

"See you later."

And that was it. Most of my trail meetings ended like this, with farewell and nothingness. I could have turned this encounter into something, given her my phone number, offered to show her some of the wonders I had found, but I didn't. Instead, I retreated into the solitude I now craved, preferring encounters with the birds and beasts, shunning the company of individuals or groups, working in isolation to improve my skills and lore.

The discipline that drew me most was animal tracking. With my very basic knowledge of the practice, I attempted to increase my awareness of an entire world around us, on the edges of the suburbs, a world we barely acknowledge except when it invades our backyards. Perhaps the family dog gets skunked or stabbed with porcupine quills. Perhaps deer graze the brush at our tree line. But a whole magical world exists beyond the margins of that backyard. Finding and entering it is surprisingly easy.

One summer day I was on a lunch break in Oxford, sitting at a picnic table on the edge of the woods. I had remained quiet and unmoving for quite a while, and suddenly a quick movement caught my eye. I narrowed my eyes, scanning the woods, and saw a brown head peeping over a log. Then, another. Two muskrats checked me out for a minute and then, convinced I was harmless, galloped through the broken woodlands towards a distant stream. I followed their tracks, marking the small details of "crumbles" and "dishes" in a notebook, and found their teepee-like home on a pond a quarter mile away.

In the spring I have often startled deer out of the brush near the trails. I'm not sure how I succeed in getting so close. Perhaps because I walk quietly on my own. Or perhaps it's because I am often the first person to walk these seldom-used trails in the cold wet early March. At any rate, the deer I usually scare out of the undergrowth are does leading me away from their fawns. They run off perhaps thirty yards and wait for me to follow. One deer in Hurd State Park along the Connecticut River kept up this charade for half a mile. I let her, knowing she was doing her best to protect her young. Following the tracks of deer became a nearly unconscious habit, leading me to places they'd bedded down, and occasionally to the surprised deer themselves.

The best time to search for animals is winter. Although fewer creatures venture from their homes in the cold, their evidence is all around. At the cessation of a snowfall, I immediately headed out into the sinus-clearing cold, through the parking lots and chain-link fences into a patch of woods. Usually, no one else had broken the fresh powder, except for the animals. I followed their tracks, tramping through the woods, finding the prints of rabbits, cats, and raccoons. I waded through the snow, enjoying the leafless skeletons of trees brushed with flakes. Finally, cross-country skiers shuffled by, waving at the strange man plodding through the fringes of the trail. I often walked alone deep into the deer-heavy forest, following my instinct through snow-choked passages in the rock. I found great slabs of basalt crackling with ice, frozen waterfalls cascading from frosted ponds, and trickles of water humming far beneath the ice. I crossed streams over wind-blown logs, using my hiking staff to balance on the slippery ice, staring through empty branches at the goose-haunted sky.

One of the best tracking experiences I had was on my birthday, the first I'd ever spent alone, when I took the Naugatuck Trail to Beacon Cap. The trail wound along a stream, past a house on the hill, crossed the creek and then split. I pondered, trying to remember the way from years before, then took the right fork. The turf was wet with new rain and snow. Dog tracks were everywhere, but no human ones. I wondered whether we had wild dogs in Connecticut and was glad that I carried bear spray. When I reached the mushroom-shaped boulder of limestone, which I had found and climbed years before, I made lunch, enjoying a view of the ridges around the Naugatuck Valley in the west and the crest of Mount Sanford in the east.

Continuing through the snow-heavy woods, I hiked a long section of the trail that had seen no human visitor for a month at least. I found squirrel and deer tracks, as well as more dog tracks. Dogs? These weren't dogs; they were coyotes! Why hadn't I seen it before? Later, I checked my field guide and became convinced. A pack of dogs gone feral in Con-necticut would have had many differently shaped and sized tracks, while these all had the same distinctive coyote look to them. I also found a set of very large prints tramping across a bald hilltop that day, but the snow had melted a bit and I didn't dare to hope that they were bear.

Despite the attraction of these diverse woodland activities, by my second autumn alone in Connecticut I had not decided on a firm purpose to my rambles. And then, one calm November day, I stepped out of my new apartment in Hamden and found it. Smelling fire in the cool air, the sweet scent of burning leaf-piles, I took my long wooden walking stick in hand, shouldered a backpack full of essentials, and tramped across the gritty parking lots, behind one of the tall, white buildings, through a fence, and down a small hill onto the long strip of the Farmington Canal Greenway. I strode happily through the last swirling leaves of the sea-son, smiling at brightly colored rollerbladers and bicyclists. Then I turned onto a small path that led through the quiet woods, hopped over a gur-gling stream, and went past a small stone dam, where a water wheel may have once stood. Ducks splashed in the water and a crow ranted from the oaks and chestnuts overhead.

The dirt path spilled out behind a warehouse, and I took the cracked macadam out to the road. This stretch had a fine grass berm and I plant-ed my walking stick in the soft earth firmly and quickly. Cars rushed by, drivers glancing curiously at this strange tramp. I suppose if I had been jogging they wouldn't have batted an eye. I stayed on the road for about a half mile, then turned left onto another road that wound up into the hills. I passed sleepy suburban houses with families raking leaves into neat piles. I waved and struggled up the hill until a small dirt tote road diverged to the right. Blue blazes on the trees told me that this was the path I wanted.

I hiked into the cinnamon forest, peering down the hill where new houses were being built. I sighed, shaking my head at the seemingly never-ending progress of civilization. But for the moment this hill was safe, and I climbed past clifflets and trees and in-between glacial erratics. Those remnants of the ice age have shaped our state, making every piece of the land unique, giving backaches to farmers, and providing gray excla-mation points to any walk in the woods.

Finding a particularly pleasant boulder, I brushed off the brown mat of leaves and set my pack on the rough stone. Digging into my pack, I pulled out a small stove, clicked metallic parts into place, and screwed the tiny top onto the fuel, pressing a button and lighting the blue flame. Then, a package of noodles and a pot appeared, which I laid aside, balancing a small titanium teapot on the metal arms. Soon it was bubbling pleasantly and I poured the water into a light metal mug. As my noodles began to cook, I sat in the perfect peaceful solitude of the forest. The far-off sound of cars occasionally drifted by. Birds became used to my presence and began their pre-winter songs once again. Leaves fell like early-season snowflakes around me and the pungent smell of compost drifted up from the valley where my home lay.

My noodles ready, I spooned them out, enjoying the scent of rich, spiced pasta. I ate slowly, savoring the combination of taste and atmosphere that only the outdoors can provide. Finishing with a handful of chocolate gorp, I packed the cooking gear away and stood up, stretching my limbs from my sojourn on the cold stone, staring through the branches at a purpling sky.

Swinging the pack up, I grabbed my gnarled stick and was off again, passing through the kind autumn woods. Down in one hollow, someone had propped chairs around a stone-ringed fire pit, forming a small camp. I smiled. I wasn't the only one who knew the peace of these in-between spaces. The path wound down the hill, joining up a worn track that must have been an old logging road. Houses appeared again, cozy and hidden in the thick forest. The dirt road spilled out onto macadam, still high on the hill. I clomped down the steep road, thinking these residents must have a hard turn with winter ice, but enjoying their semi-isolation here from the thick omnipresent suburbia of Connecticut. Turning onto a busier road, still following the blue blazes of the Quinnipiac Trail, I hunched toward the metal barriers, avoiding the rushing cars. But after only a short stretch, I was back onto the Greenway again, turning south towards home. I sauntered slowly, watching birds and chatting with other walkers.

Not feeling quite finished, I struck off into the forest about a mile from home. I explored a stream, which a hundred years ago had been called Shepherd's Brook, treading carefully over mossy rocks and tree roots. I discovered an old platform, perhaps left from the canal days. I paused here and there, searching for animal signs, finding bird tracks in the mud and rodent holes near the banks. Then I moved further into the woods, past the rusting frame of an old bed, along a backwater. Ducks burst from the stream, flying south. Woodchucks and moles were no doubt burrowing deeper, preparing for the winter. Toads and turtles had already disappeared into the mire. Shimmering spiderwebs joined the rosy and amber leaves of birches, maples, and oaks. Gray squirrels dashed back and forth, cheeks full of acorns. Brisk breezes caused me to stuff my hands in my pockets, but the cool air was pleasant, not uncomfortable. Afternoon settled into evening, the sky hazy and diffuse. Ahead of me I spotted a mossy glade, where orange leaves spiraled slowly to the green earth, and I knew I had found what I was searching for. All those activities were only excuses, and this was the true reward, a day on foot with the chance to find a secret place, like the lost play-forests of childhood blown up to marvelous proportions.

Stopping there in the hidden space between the suburbs, barely a mile from my doorstep, I sat quietly in the center of a group of small hemlock trees, hunched below larger maples. Beams of golden sunlight streamed horizontally through gaps in the gnarled conifers, illuminating a pool of water, a tuft of grass, and the remnants of a stone wall, as magical and beautiful as any spot on earth.

Chapter Four

Ancient Pathways

O n a warm Thursday in March, I parked at the junction of Route 68 and 157 to explore a section of the Mattabesett Trail. *The Connecticut Walk Book* claimed that the blue blazes crossed the two-hundred-fifty-year-old Wadsworth Farm Road, from Wallingford to Durham, which George Washington had used in 1775 and 1789. I climbed the back side of the long traprock ridge, fording streams and picking my way through the remnants of some sort of selective logging. A few patches of snow lingered on the north faces of cliffs, but the first ferns and skunk cabbages already poked out of the wet earth. I passed deer tracks and scat, a possible bobcat print, and human boot prints at least a day old. I was alone in the bare March forest. This was the best time to search for archaeological vestiges, after the winter snows, but before the explosion of spring leaves that obscured stone walls and foundations.

One of the astonishing aspects of New England is its age. In Connecticut and its neighbors, the legions of stone boundaries and ruins from the first few hundred years of European colonization are a rare treat for many Americans. They allow us to read the history on the landscape, feel the patterns of ancient farmlands, and touch a piece of the past. When I first began my journeys in the forests of Connecticut, I was baffled as to why people had built stone walls through the forests. Perhaps this was a bit naïve. But I quickly understood that the walls had existed before the trees, that once nearly all the trees between the Atlantic and the Mississippi had been cut down. And in New England, they had been logged several times. These radical changes made it difficult to find the traces of our history, but not impossible.

The majority of these stone walls had been constructed in the early 1800's, though some were started earlier or completed later. The farm pastures came complete with "wolf" or pasture trees, those lone giants that often provided shade for animals and farmers, some of which survive today, looking strangely out of place in our young forests. Many times I had found an old oak spreading its branches wide in a tightly-packed forest and been confused, until I learned how these anomalies came to be.

As I reached the narrow plateau, which dropped off suddenly to farms and lakes far below, I wondered what form this ancient road would take. Would it be flanked by stone walls, like the well-preserved roads scattered across our state? Would it be a sunken lane, with dikes on each side, like those common in England? Excitedly, I pushed along the ridge, then dropped into a hanging valley, where I was sure the road must be. I had already crossed several fairly new logging roads, probably cut in the past thirty years, and certainly in the last hundred. Now I passed more, while loud pops from a nearby firing range echoed off the cliffs and boulders. But nothing appeared.

Maybe this wasn't the location. I reminded myself that woods time was slow time, that a mile in the forest was like three on the pavement. I kept walking, hungry now, searching for this mysterious pathway, thinking back to the first place I discovered a great concentration of these archaic traces, near my home in Hamden.

My friends from Pennsylvania, Ryan and Jenifer, walked with me on a March day two years earlier, up the paved Farmington Canal Greenway, planning on making a giant loop back to my apartment. The canal was a result of a crazily ambitious plan to create a channel from New Haven to Lake Memphremagog on the Canadian border. It never got past Northampton, Massachusetts, though that eighty-seven mile accomplishment seems quite enough today. The farmers and landholders whose lands were crossed by this long scar hated it, and the railroads took over shortly afterwards

Ryan was a friend from graduate school, and often my only connection with the outside world. He and I corresponded often, discussing and arguing, sharing and learning. He and his wife Jenifer knew that I was alone here and made biannual trips to alleviate this condition. He introduced me to the art of weightlifting, and I felt I had to return the favor in some way, so I always planned an interesting walk, though they rarely hiked in Pennsylvania, despite being in better physical shape than me. She was a yoga teacher; he had been a runner in college, and now huge muscles wrapped around his legs, the product of years of heavy squats.

This time, we entered Brookvale Town Park and tramped up the slopes after looking at peacocks and turkeys in the small wildlife enclave. Somewhere along the dirt path we crossed into a section of Naugatuck State Forest, where stone walls began to appear crossing the blazed trail. But this was only the beginning. The ruins of an ancient village crumbled in the silent wood. Leaves were not on the trees yet, the day was warm and bright, and we could see properties marked off in definitive subdivisions. Ryan and Jenifer expressed astonishment at the old road with stone walls on each side, just wide enough for a carriage. We walked on top of one of the walls, avoiding large puddles of spring run-off, then stopped and ate lunch on a fallen tree, munching apples and pistachios. I had taken a few other people through this stretch of inviting woods, but never walked here all the way from my house and made the eleven-mile circuit. Still, as we sat there in the remains of a fallen community, I could feel the history seeping through my bootsoles.

Property walls continually crisscrossed the path as we trundled down through the area of the state forest where logging was taking place. Signs proclaimed, "It's for the birds!" —insisting that the logging operation benefited the ecosystem. The three of us laughed at the self-serving rhetoric, but understood that such change would always take place, that permanence was an illusion, and indeed years later I would return to find large stands of these hardwoods gone. We discussed childhood haunts that had disappeared under the bulldozer, reminiscing sadly. We passed an old YMCA building with cracking tennis courts and a leaf-encrusted pool, isolated out here at the end of a long country road.

We marched down that road, taking the path in reverse I would take years later on my first hike across the state. Then we entered the woods, passing more pine groves and stone walls, one which dove down the side of a hill at seventy degrees. A small foundation lay nearly hidden in the leaves, almost directly underneath a set of high-tension wires. "It's so small!" Ryan wondered and Jenifer laughingly explained that our modern houses were palaces in comparison to the humble abodes of former times.

We walked a hemlock forest path covered with brown leaves, past a radio tower, underneath a huge pylon and a cable that swayed in the wind. Another house ruin crumbled on a ledge looking west, a tall chimney and walled room creating a wonderful spot, where someone from the nearby community had set up camp, using a rotting mattress and makeshift tables. Then, we clambered down into a valley, across a road, and onto High Rock, where I had seen a black snake and bobcat years before, and southerly views of the New Haven took us back to my home. Ryan and Jenifer had never seen so many ruins before, and we talked all night about the lost world all around us, where the ghosts of pioneers and Indians did battle for the spoils of an alien landscape...

On the Mattabesett Trail that March day two years later, the trail dropped down from the ridge and turned east. I could see out over a deep blue lake. The afternoon sun sparkled across it and on passing cars below. Cars? A road split the ridge, hugging the shore of the lake. I studied the map and found to my amusement that I had traveled almost four miles, well past the supposed eighteenth century road. Puzzled, I found a rock on the edge of the steep hill and boiled tea. I ate a hearty lunch of summer sausage, hard cheese, and dried blueberries. I studied the map and shrugged. How did I miss a road? I knew what I was looking for; I had plenty of experience with these colonial ruins. I had visited and studied innumerable stone walls, hundreds of foundation holes, and at least seven abandoned towns on my hikes around the state, like Millington Green, an old lumber town near the Connecticut River.

But the most famous and persistent of these ghostly remnants is Dudleytown. When trying to find information about this legendary village, a dedicated researcher will only find frustration. Stories about both the origin of town and its curse vary widely depending on the source. Some legends attribute the town's name to the Dudley family of England, cursed due to their involvement in two scandals that rocked the British crown during the 1500s. The hilltop town itself had been settled in the early 1700s, though actual dates are difficult to pin down. Then, in the early 1800s, something had happened, a murder, a suicide, a massacre. Nothing is certain. The town could have failed due to poor soil, to livestock plagues, or to a resounding curse that doomed the village. No one is sure, but legends abound. Supposedly no birds live in the ruins. Strange voices call to visitors from the trees. At night, brave local kids see ghostly figures chopping wood and sweeping eroded doorsteps.

Later, I would try to take a student group up Dark Entry Road to this mysterious place, and be rebuffed. Police officers told me not to attempt it, as the local owners would call them and they would be forced to arrest us for trespassing, even though one of our blue trails winds directly through the ruins. And really, who could blame them? Hundreds of tourists each year leave not only garbage, but evidence of strange witchy rituals, sprinkled about the adjoining private lands high on the mountain.

After a view of that strange hilltop from the top of the nearby Mohawk Mountain one autumn day, I headed down into the old-growth of the Cathedral Pines. One shorn pine loomed over the trailhead like a giant telephone pole, stripped by an unlucky tornado. These pines were the progeny of the ancient groves that had greeted early Europeans, towering over all other northeastern trees. Eight feet wide and over two-hundred feet high, they were the first to fall to early loggers for use as ship masts. Today a pine half the age and height is deemed impressive in Connecticut and these few groves in Cornwall are among the best.

I walked through the wide, church-like spaces on the Mohawk trail, surveying curiously. And there, in the midst of the brown, soft-needle forest I found the evidence of an old farm, more ancient even than those ancient trees. More ancient still was the trail itself, possibly part of the old path worn by the moccasins of the Mohawks as they made the rounds collecting tribute from their neighbors. These trails were rare now, but only because so many of them had been in such convenient places that the settlers paved over them. We now drive our combustion-engine vehicles along those old Indian roads, unaware of the bold feet that began them.

One of the great places in Connecticut to see the evidence of the past is Hartman Park in Lyme, which had been donated privately, a rare example of historical conservation. I followed the suggested trail in a hiking guide during the black and white month of February, once again to see the ruins more clearly. Beautiful carpets of dead leaves covered the ground and crunched pleasantly beneath my bootsoles. Foundations flanked by long stone barriers peeked out of the brown leaves on the glaciated hillsides. The walls stretched in unusual patterns and I puzzled over the property line schemes, trying to map the village. Round and square heaps of stones, shoulder-high and about ten feet in circumference, dotted the flatter areas. I puzzled over these, too, unsure if they were tumbled remains of houses or piles created later by loggers. Some of the rock walls and buildings had been incorporated into the natural landscape, using boulders and ledges. Large American hornbeam trees now sprouted from many of them, a reminder of the generations between.

The jewel of the park is a much larger ruin, called Three Chimneys, which the guidebook speculates is one of a series of forts built by the Puritan settlers of Saybrook Colony in 1634. If so, it would be miraculous. Even if not, it is a curious structure that demands careful study and attention, even by a casual walker. A fairly large stone perimeter, six feet in height at some points, hems in a hilltop, three crumbled chimneys near the center giving the site its name. The piles of stones I had seen earlier were larger and more numerous within the fort's ellipse. Small oven-like openings created with large flat stones had been built into the steeper part of the hillside. After examination, I decided that this indeed must have been a fort, though not necessarily the one the book described.

Many glacial erratics were also scattered throughout Hartman Park, including "the snout," a nose-like projection formed when the lower part of a boulder fell away. Small caves dropped into the leaf-litter underneath minor moraines. A transmission corridor cut through the heart of the park, rolling over the hills like the crashpath of a meteor. These corridors have actually become important wildlife habitats in New England, due to the lack of other scrub and meadow areas.

In this powerline clearing, a stream skated over long areas of flat slate in its tumble down the slope. Near the access corridor, an ancient graveyard hid behind a stubby stone wall. The gravestones were small and unmarked, but clearly part of a rural farming cemetery. I wondered what pioneer family or community had buried their dead here, solemnly placing crude headstones over these casualties of harsh New England winters or enemy aggression. What farmers heaved these stones? And more tangibly, I wondered how this wonderful piece of history had been left untouched. As I left Hartman Park, I wondered how modern life would be if these reminders of the past were everywhere, so that we could not escape our heritage, so that each step we took echoed on the foundations of antiquity.

This thought was in my mind as I wandered back along the Mattabesett toward the hypothetical location of another ancient pathway. I wanted to tread on ground made holy by the myths of this land. Along the way, past hollow trees filled with hibernating squirrels, I paid close attention to the erosion-resistant traprock topography, peeking over the cliffs to estimate height-of-land, and counting the small bluffs. Finally, I arrived at what I was sure must be the place.

A flat track, indistinguishable from the web of tote roads, ran perpendicular to the trail, and indeed most of the other paths. It curved less than the haphazard logging trails, and ran directly through the lowest notch in the hills. I studied the lines of the map carefully. I walked west on the indeterminate road to see where it sloped down towards the lake and farms. This was the one place where the jagged ridge did not plunge steeply to the flatlands below. One last test…I climbed the adjoining hill and peered west. I could see no evidence of distant Wallingford, but could see the ridges on each side of the Quinnipiac River Valley. Struggling to the other flank of the hill, I looked east. The historic town of Durham poked little white house-heads above the trees. This was it – the fabled road George Washington traveled on. But it was barely there! No stone walls, no dikes, no trace of its proud history remained. Perhaps it was better preserved elsewhere. But here it was disappearing into the timber like a sad ghost. I couldn't picture the past here the way I could in the Naugatuck State Forest or Hartman Park. I sighed and shouldered my pack. I had better get moving; I had a lot to see before it was lost forever.

Chapter Five

My First Struggle Across Connecticut

A friend named Lauren drove me to the base of West Rock, near where I taught English at Southern Connecticut State University. We hiked to the top together, but that was as far as she was going. I was about to walk across Connecticut by myself. Rain began slashing down—an inauspicious start. We said goodbye after huddling under the small pavilion and taking pictures in the stone picnic area. Then I set off. My backpack sat heavily on my hips and shoulders, a huge mass, inescapable, upwards of fifty pounds, full of food, water, extra clothes, a Primus stove, cooking gear, a tent and tarp, emergency gear of all sorts, and a leather-bound journal. I came prepared for the rain, with a hooded jacket and baseball cap. My green quick-dry pants and hiking staff completed the list. I was ready to hike from Long Island Sound to Massachusetts border, something I had considered ever since I traced the beautifully long north-south paths in the *Connecticut Walk Book*.

This wonderful trail system had been conceived in 1929 and by 1937, four hundred miles of trails had been developed, beginning with the Quinnipiac Trail. Now there are seven hundred miles maintained by Connecticut Forest and Park Association volunteers, though encroaching development always threatens sections in both rural and urban areas.

Since I have started walking the trails, new sections have opened, others have been rerouted, and still others have disappeared. The original plan of following the Metacomet Trail all the way was hampered by a huge "closed" section of the trail north of Meriden.

I had spent over a hundred hours preparing for this moment, which was a bit ridiculous. I pored over topographical maps, searched the internet for motels and campgrounds, and drove back and forth across our state, road maps in hand, scoping out the possible routes. I wrote a flyer to gain possible support from my students or colleagues, giving my trek the ambitious title: "Space Between the Suburbs." The original plan was to head more or less straight north from West Rock using the blue trail system as much as possible. However, searches for lodging along the way came up with nil, leading to long days of confused frustration. Beautiful long footpaths stretched across the state, but camping was forbidden. Motels and hotels bunched close to the highways, of course. Finally, switching my route slightly to the west, I was able to chart a suitable outline, though it used too many roads, at least to my thinking then. The Connecticut Department of Environmental Protection granted me permission to camp along the Tunxis Trail and the strategy was complete, though much changed from my original sketch.

Now, on a stormy May day, these hopefully logical plans were about to be put to the test. Steeling myself against the downpour, I marched along the road atop West Rock until it veered off. Then, I took the path above the Merritt Parkway and through wet green grass. Cars zoomed by below, their echoes seeming to come from the bowels of the earth. Distracted, I nearly tripped over a yellow and brown leopard patterned box turtle. A herd of at least ten deer stared at me from a wooded hillock. Suddenly, the rain was forgotten and I was in the magical forest-world again. I tramped by in misty silence, following blue splashes of paint on the maples and elms.

I passed the famous "Judges Cave," where two of the judges who had ordered the death of England's Charles the First had fled after the Restoration of the monarchy in 1660. William Goffe and Edward Whalley had hidden at the cave and been brought food by sympathetic townsfolk, who did what they could to slow down the king's officers who were hot on the trail of the two judges turned criminals. Claiming a panther had terrified them in the night, they later fled to the farm of Mr. Sperry in

Woodbridge, near the present-day site of the famous Whitlock's Book Barn, then on to Milford and Massachusetts, where they spent the rest of their lives in hiding. These two men were called "regicides" for their crime and gave that name to the trail I was walking that cold morning.

I had hiked West Rock several times, once by myself, once with Ryan and Jenifer, and once with a friend named Robin. I had also attempted to bring my SCSU English classes up the craggy hill for their final exam. But they had complained and some had not even completed the short walk, so I abandoned the idea after that first try. The area around Lake Wintergreen was popular, but much of the back ridge was unused. One day, I had clambered up the hill to the clearing above the city and ate my lunch. Looking towards Sleeping Giant, I could see smoke rising from three points in the forest. I puzzled over that for a while. The next day, I found out that some maniac had intentionally set the fires, which fortunately had been controlled. Hiking a long loop with Robin, we had witnessed a second fire in the downtown area of New Haven. "Perhaps we ought to install the old fire-tower customs again," I had suggested.

The dirt path reached a disintegrating park road along the top of the wooded ridge, a cyclists' paradise providing miles of perfect biking. For me, choosing to pound across the macadam rather than to weave through the woods allowed me to eat the distance more quickly, but my feet began to shout at me. The first junction at High Rock appeared in a mere two-and-a-half hours. I clambered upward, breathing heavily, doubts assailing me. Low clouds rolled around me, filling the valleys beyond. My feet and legs burned. "Will I even make it through day one? Am I walking too fast?" I asked myself. "What am I doing here in Connecticut, walking this path?"

These sorts of questions assail every walker and the walker may be the only one qualified to answer it. Connecticut has two famous writers who were also prodigious walkers. The twentieth-century poet Wallace Stevens found his answers in a daily walk to his job in Hartford. On his long trek from West Hartford, he would compose poems in his head, later writing them down and becoming one of the century's great poets of ideas. Mark Twain is perhaps our most famous writer, and he himself was a constant walker, finding peace and wisdom in long rambles at home and abroad. Both wrote of their love of walking, though I'm not sure either conceived of walking quite in the way I was now undertaking it. In fact, Twain wrote in *A Tramp Abroad* that "the true charm of pedestrian-ism does not lie in the walking, or in the scenery, but in the talking. The walking is good to time the movement of the tongue by, and to keep the blood and the brain stirred up and active; the scenery and the woodsy smells are good to bear in upon a man an unconscious and unobtrusive charm and solace to eye and soul and sense; but the supreme pleasure comes from the talk. It is no matter whether one talks wisdom or non-sense, the case is the same, the bulk of the enjoyment lies in the wagging of the gladsome jaw and the flapping of the sympathetic ear."[1]

One Connecticut resident who might have thought of walking in my way, however, was John Ledyard of Groton, born in 1751. He carved his own canoe and paddled down the Connecticut River from Dartmouth, he sailed with Captain Cook on the discovery of Hawaii, and visited countries as varied as China, Gibraltar, and the West Indies. His own journey on foot was from Stockholm, Sweden to St. Petersburg, Russia: 1400 miles! From there he continued east to Irktusk, but was kicked out of Russia before completing his mission—to reach the Pacific Northwest of North America via Siberia. His walks made my more modest attempts look a lot less "crazy."

After High Rock, I traveled over the western section of the Quin-nipiac Trail. The rain finally stopped, but mist hung like curtains in the semi-forested neighborhoods. I made it to the roads by the YMCA, my first planned campsite, at two-thirty, very early. But the woods were soaked, the ground muddy and cold, and I groaned with thoughts of the long, wet hours ahead. Nearby, a pleasant-looking middle-aged woman was talking to the mailman.

"Excuse me. Would you mind if I looked at your phone book?" I asked, hoping I didn't appear too disreputable in my soggy hiking clothes.

"Of course not! Come inside and use the phone." She smiled and waved me in.

I waffled, but then put down my pack and accepted her hospitality. Her husband greeted me and we all began talking about my hike and about their son, who attended college in the area. I made my call and got the very last room at the Cheshire Welcome Inn; it was Memorial Day weekend and the price had unfortunately ballooned. Still, I didn't want to sleep in the chilly, soaked outdoors tonight, knowing the long days I had ahead.

While we chatted, the kind couple gave me a soda to drink and another for the road. I smiled as I trundled down the road and into the Naugatuck State Forest. These encounters seemed to be rarer and rarer, with people valuing their privacy and security above all else. These two generous citizens practically invited me to put up the tent in their back yard.

I studied the map and found to my dismay that this detour added four miles to my total distance. I sighed, but hoped the benefits outweighed the problems. So, I continued past Mount Sanford, which I climbed once with a colleague from Southern Connecticut State University, Chris. We had found a box nailed to a tree with a journal for hikers' notes. These were appearing all over the state, along with GPS treasure troves. "Anything that gets people into the forest is okay in my book." I muttered, talking to myself already, surely not a good sign.

Rain began splattering the leaves again, seemingly supporting the cowardly decision I had just made. I plodded through the stone-walled roads and ran into the only person on the trails I'd seen all day, a biker splashing across the swollen streams, braving the downpour. Then I took the Farmington Canal Greenway for a mile or two, avoiding a wandering drunk who was stumbling back and forth along the Greenway in the rain with a paper-bagged bottle. I saluted him as I passed, not wanting to seem rude. He goggled at me as if I was a ghost.

My mother and I had walked for quite a way along this canal route, heading south back to my house. I tried to explain my love of walking, telling her of noodle lunches and boulders. I think she understood that afternoon. But this day three years later, as my feet began to hurt and my skin shriveled with dampness, I began questioning those restless urges in my feet, suspecting myself of prideful hubris.

I cut across a suburban lane to Route 10, passing a nursery and greenhouse, finally reaching the strip-mall area where the fancy brown and white sign of the Cheshire Motor Inn waited. A huge flag drooped in the heavy rain. I checked in, took a shower, and cooked a late lunch. My gear unfolded and draped throughout the heated room and I prayed it would dry by tomorrow. I felt a little disappointed in myself for not camping, and more so when I ordered a pizza, very civilized. Later, I watched empty hours of television, disgusted with my lack of industry and fortitude, traits the Yankees of old Connecticut had in abundance.

Before going to sleep, I found that I had acquired a fine blister on my big toe, no doubt from all the rain, the extra mileage, and the macadam. Little did I know that this minor chink in my hiking armor was only the beginning.

On my map, day two was an all-road walking stage, with an optional detour on the southernmost section of the Tunxis Trail. I left the Motor Inn at 8:30 and stopped at the 7-11 for a pastry and Gatorade breakfast. Gorged, I stumbled through Cheshire on Routes 10 and 68, passing an ancient cemetery full of huge purple azaleas. I noticed that the tree species along the roads have even less unity than the young New England forests. My thighs started to chafe in my loose hiking pants and I continued walking with a wider gait, like a duck. I reached the Notch, which I was supposed to be entering from the south instead of the east, and turned north on Moss Farms Road. The walking there was pleasant despite various mongrels barking furiously from their yard-chains. I turned on Jarvis and then onto Marion, exchanging friendly hellos with suburban folk working in their yards and walking dogs. Near a large pond, a line of parental geese led goslings across the farmlands for a noontime dip. Somewhere along this endless straightaway is where the weight started to get to me. As I waded for miles up through western Southington, my left knee began bothering me a little, no doubt from the ridiculous duck walk I had adopted. Having no choice but to continue, I had to stop quite often to rest as the joint worsened.

I passed a maroon house draped in flags, with a white picket fence set back from the road like a tiny patriotic citadel. Then, a delightful rill flowed out of the hills towards the road, bordered by fields of daisies, crossed by a small red bridge near a small red barn. "Good luck!" A shocked man at a horse farm told me when I related my goal. Shortly after that encounter the trail turned off to the left, climbing a gentle traprock ridge which at that moment seemed like Mount Everest. No way was I taking that option. I continued and soon stumbled past the green fields of Briarwood College and the fortress of Lake Compounce. The red and yellow spiral of one of the rides peeked over the high fence. I tramped by, pausing to peer through the chain links at groups of identically dressed amusement park workers, who milled around preparing for the summer season. Perhaps I had started too early. The nights were still cold and the spring clouds had certainly not finished their annual deluge.

I stopped more frequently, rubbing my aching legs anxiously. Finally, the suburban sprawl gave way to the stoplights and macadam lots of Bristol. I found precious few sidewalks that day, and grumpily cursed our car-centered culture that denied people the use of their own feet. These residents could not walk from their own doorsteps without considering the pitfalls of traveling in the open street. Lunch occurred at 3:30 p.m. at Dunkin Donuts—a Connecticut tradition that I decided to pay homage to. I gulped down a quart of milk and it never tasted so sweet and refreshing. After consulting my maps, I found the road that led up to Chimney Crest Manor. Though accurate, the topographical map had unfortunately not prepared me for the incredible gradient of the hill at the center of town, which nearly killed me in my weakened state. I stopped frequently and was asked "are you all right?" by a man strangely watering his immaculate lawn, despite yesterday's monsoon. I shrugged uncertainly and as skateboarding teenagers slid past me down the dangerous hill, I reached my destination, which was a bit expensive for a weary foot traveler. However, it happened to be the only resting place along the direct northern route. Any motels would require several miles of side-tracking, something I certainly could afford much less.

The Manor itself was a veritable castle, surrounded by trees and a brick fence, with all the trapping of the finest bed and breakfasts. The bedroom had a view east to the Farmington Ridge, my original plan of attack. Day two gave me a good view of suburban Connecticut, with its little gardens and lawn ornaments, its bird feeders and colorful mailboxes, the unbroken sea of residences that blankets the center of our state. But I had already come an astonishing thirty-five miles, crushed by a bursting backpack. As I ordered another pizza, the doubts that had plagued me for two days attacked again and made me wonder if I had chosen the wrong route after all. Today had been brutally long and I felt crippled as I tumbled into troubled sleep.

Chapter Six

Failure at New Hartford

I stayed at the picturesque Chimney Crest Manor the next day. Outside, the rain poured down in sheets of blinding white, blanketing the breathtaking Tudor-style mansion. Inside, flagstoned floors, carved wood paneling, and ancient chairs completed the castle effect. I relaxed my aching legs on their ultra-soft couch, wrote bad poetry, watched bad television, read magazines and books, and talked to the owners, Dan and Cynthia. I enjoyed my breather day for the most part, but occasionally glanced out the window through the downpour at the green rectangle of the backyard. Doubts continued to creep in: whether I was really cut out for the tramping life, whether I had the constitution, and whether I even possessed a fraction of the necessary willpower.

I thought about the famous Leatherman, whose eponymous cave above the Naugatuck River I had explored a few years before. This fascinating character, named Jules Bourglay, had emigrated from France due to some mischance or crime. The first report of his activities was in 1862, and he quickly became a local legend. He made a 34 day walking circuit through a section of Connecticut and New York, staying in caves along the way, refusing offers from farmers to stay in houses or barns. He wore a stitched suit of all leather, as heavy as the pack I carried, and made and sold leather implements, but what stuck with me about the story was his stubbornness, his will. I admired this man's courage and fortitude and in some small way wanted to honor him.

Day two had been much harder than expected. My left thigh hurt and my right calf cramped up horribly as I was resting at the bed and breakfast. I counted five blisters now, including one that had blown up like a balloon the size of a sixth toe. I was in constant pain, even when not moving, requiring the constant use of ibuprofen. I decided that the weight of the pack was prohibitive, but couldn't choose anything to leave behind. I probably had too many cold-weather clothes, shirts, and socks. The packages of noodles and oatmeal were certainly too numerous, lying idle while I devoured restaurant food. I feared that I couldn't finish and would need more than this one break day.

I resolved to deal with the blisters. My feet became a patchwork of bandages and moleskin which evolved and improved throughout the rest day. My knees, however, were another story. I worried that I was doing some sort of lasting damage, but I was determined to go through with this plan. As Thoreau said in his famous essay on walking, "If you are ready to leave father and mother and brother and sister, and wife and child and friends, and never see them again, —if you have paid your debts, and made your will, and settled all your affairs, and are a free man, then you are ready for a walk."[1] I held to this idea, convinced that my solitary push through pain was the only way. I ate through some of my unused food while relaxing in the tranquil living room of the Manor, but couldn't bring myself to throw the rest of it away. For dinner I ordered food once again, this time toning down the grease factor with a sandwich. Dan offered to drive me to a nearby restaurant, but I stubbornly chose to remain an all-foot traveler.

The morning of the fourth day shone sunny and wet. I ate a generous English breakfast with Cynthia, though I got started a bit later than I would have liked. Heading down the huge hill in the center of Bristol through the dripping town park, I hummed a morning walking song. So far, so good. Still, I cautiously stopped at Walgreens and picked up a knee brace, wondering if it would do any good. I decided to try not to think about the pain. As the suburbs slowly fell away, a stream rushed by with yesterday's rain. A small white bridge crossed it, connecting two back-yards. I wonder at this oddity – are they friends or family? Why should

I be more surprised by this than by two neighbors putting up a high wall between them?

I headed up Jerome Street for a couple miles, then turned left on the aptly named Shrub to the Barnes Nature Center, which was unfortunately closed. I took a photo of myself mirrored in the giant flag-draped window. I happily re-entered the divine woods here, following the Tunxis Trail's blue blazes, wondering if the trail had been used by the native Tunxis tribe when they dominated the area. The footpath overflowed with ferns and skunk cabbage, crossing and re-crossing a meandering stream on wooden planks. Pine trees swayed above me, the stream below me teemed with life, and the world shone green, fabulously green. Everything was complete and vibrating with me in molecular tandem. I could hear the god-whispers of leaves in the wind and swore that whatever the fate of this foolish tramp across Connecticut, the demons of pain and fear would not defeat me.

These noble thoughts quickly turned to tar as the trail exited onto the busy Route 69 over an old-fashioned stile. After a long hill, I dove back into the deliciously cool forest again, heading out of Bristol and into Burlington. The trail was a bit disappointing, being mostly on woods roads, which rolled up and down, up and down. A sapling bent over the trail like an arch at one point; I walked right under it without hunching. Occasionally, I spotted a foundation or old wall buried in the trees. I encountered a man sweeping the paths with a metal detector and realized that other than the biker on day one, I had met no one else on any of the trails. I guess May was too cold and rainy for most. "They're smarter than I am," I muttered to myself.

The path had a gap of two miles, where I entered the quaint Burlington town center. Exhausted again, I caved and stopped at a fine restaurant, which unfortunately added several hundred yards to my distance. Even this small detour had me to the point of despair. I politely asked for a table and sat across from my giant blue backpack. Other patrons stared at me curiously and I related my journey to the incredulous waitstaff. I surprisingly couldn't eat the entire meal, but this may have been due to the two pitchers of water I gulped down. Strangely unsatisfied, I plodded on, finding the entrance to the Tunxis Trail a mile up an empty country road.

As the afternoon lengthened, I passed several farms with fresh shoots poking from the tilled earth. Giant pines loomed over the endless brown logging roads, filling the day with unnatural darkness. Black, heavy clouds hung over a large swamp, where leafless bushes disintegrated in the sloppy mud. A large pasture spattered with white, fluffy dandelions. Constant birdsong followed me and toads and chipmunks scampered along the edges of the path, as if encouraging me to leave it. Disturbingly, my quadriceps began to go numb somewhere near the Nepaug Reservoir.

Signs that read "Failure to remain on blue trail constitutes trespassing" haunted every turning. Why not open more water-supply roads? Why not make networks for walking, connecting the greenways with the blue trails? Of course, private property laws hinder this process. But who was I to complain of all this private land? That's what I wanted on my walks – privacy. I could not throw this stone. Still, these trails are public lands, created as part of our common heritage. We are part owners of every foot of trail; they are our home.

These conflicting thoughts merely made my problems more acute. William Hazlitt wrote in "On Going A Journey," "give me the clear blue sky over my head, and the green turf beneath my feet, a winding road before me, and a three hours march to dinner."[2] Had Hazlitt walked forty miles before this with a heavy pack? Was my negative attitude due to the fact that I was on a path of few choices? I couldn't have stopped in Burlington that day, because there were no inns or motels. I could camp in these woods illegally, but did not feel like breaking the law. Bitterness welled up, but I had no one to vent my spleen at. I cursed my feet, my legs, my stupidity at planning this nightmare walk. And when I found myself in the home stretch near the gorge of Satan's Kingdom, I didn't even stop to consider the campsite the DEP had granted me. I plodded on an extra two miles to the Alcove Motel on Route 4. After unpacking everything, I hobbled over to the nearby grocery store and bought more supplies, sure I was not going to have the energy to cook that night. I cursed my over-planning—bags of uncooked pasta stared at me from the pile on the floor. Not to mention the unused tent and sleeping bag.

I examined my feet, which were now a horrifying mess, bubbling with multiple blisters. Huge balloons of pain pushed my big toe from the second, separating them at an extreme angle. More blisters wrapped around the top of my toes, red with infection around the tender edges. But the unrelenting numbness in my left thigh is what really scared me. What if this condition was permanent? I studied the map: twenty miles to go to the campground in Massachusetts, with no options for sleeping except camping. At least that would justify carrying all this gear for fifty miles. But the hills on the map laughed at my hubris; the guidebook described them as some of the toughest in the state. I couldn't make it in one day, and if my legs gave out, I had little recourse. I realized now that the route was flawed, that despite dozens of hours of planning, I had miscalculated the effect the burdensome pack would have on my body.

I could hear water rushing by in the nearby Satan's Kingdom Gorge, which was formed by intense geological pressures cutting through mountains that once towered here, and is now known as some of the best rafting in Connecticut. But during the late 1700s this area was a hideaway for criminals and outlaws. And now, I was hiding, too – from myself, my own weakness, my ambitions and plans. It was time to face up to some hard facts about this solitary outlaw attitude. It was not about adventure, but somehow an evasion.

As rain began pounding again outside, I decided with disgust that discretion was the better part of valor. The rain had made the woods a sloppy mess for camping, not to mention unpleasant for hiking. I thought of more persistent long-distance hikers, like those who hiked the entire Appalachian Trail, and measured myself against their strength. I seemed quite pathetic and groaned audibly in despair. And that was the final straw—the walk was no longer fun. It had become a death march, a walk for the sake of finishing, rather than something I enjoyed. I called my father and he drove all the way from Pennsylvania the next morning and generously picked me up without a qualm.

I got back on the horse a few weeks later, ironically hiking a loop in the western section of my new archenemy the Tunxis Trail. I rambled over the famed "mile of ledges" and helped a lost couple find their way. I explored the "Tory Den," haven of British loyalists during the Revolutionary War. I cooked lunch on a log in the gentle woodlands, my struggle forgotten, with only love for the emerald land of my failure.

Most people think of New England in the autumn: red and brown leaves spiraling down country lanes, the smell of bonfires and pumpkins, and the first hints of frosty air sweeping off the hills. Others remember winter: long evenings by cozy firesides, fresh snow piling on the windowsill, or a village square blanketed in white. There are other colors, as well: the rich browns of November, the gray tones of February, the blues of August. But for a walker, Connecticut is somehow always green: the brilliant new leaves after a spring storm, the sunlit summer grass, and the countless waving willow reeds. If my failure at New Hartford taught me anything, it was that no fire of pain or doubt could ever burn that color away.

Chapter Seven

The Birds and the Silence

Much as I hate to admit it, Connecticut is not the best state for views. We do not have many open ridges or cliffs, due mainly to the prodigious forests that now cover both highlands and lowlands. I'm certainly not going to complain about that. But amongst our wooded kingdom, a few lonely crests surface, and the overall lack makes us walkers appreciate them all the more. I search for these lofty apertures with preoccupied regularity, but the reasons are somewhat of a mystery.

Many would argue that the best vista in the state is from Heublein Tower on Talcott Mountain north of Hartford, the first public look-out tower in the United States. Talcott Mountain is one of the high points of the Metacomet Ridge, which divides Connecticut's central valley in two, providing a huge obstacle for early settlers of Hartford and New Haven who wanted to trade. The ridge was formed by volcanic activity that left it harder than the surrounding brownstone, which eroded away into soil, leaving this mighty crinkle in the earth's surface. All around the ridge, the rich alluvial plain provided and still provides sustenance for farmers. I saw many of these farms, most of them tobacco, as I drove up the steep road one gorgeous summer day.

I knew about this ridge from early explorations, but didn't climb Heublein Tower until I had lived in Connecticut for three years. I parked across from Penwood Park in a overpacked lot, noting the strange popularity of this walk. I found out why soon enough: my car had done the serious work and barely any hill remained to climb. As the trail hit a traprock ridge, a view from the cliff over the meandering Farmington River opened to the west. Down the hill at the nearby bridge lives the Pinchot sycamore, the largest tree in Connecticut, like a giant cupped hand with dozens of fingers, mottled white and gray. But the real bonus of this walk waited at the tower. I paid a small fee and climbed up and up the worn steps, finally popping up into the glass-encircled top-bulb. Immediately, I spun around wildly. On this clear summer day, I could see south across our beautiful state to the far-off ridge of Sleeping Giant. Directly below were the twin cities of Hartford and Springfield, seemingly adjoining each other, linked by the short strip of Interstate 91. The view stretched north across Massachusetts to the shoulders of Mount Tom and beyond. East and west, ranges of green hills rolled away, distances unlike anything I had thought possible in southern New England. The view was truly magnificent, giving a sense of geographical space that burned onto my brain like a tattoo. And that is certainly one reason to find these viewpoints and outlooks, the satisfaction of seeing a giant's blueprint, a living map.

Other towers dot the state, but one I had always wanted to try only a few miles north of my house in Hamden, the heroically named Castle Craig in Meriden. So, on a rare weekday off, I parked near a large pond, where dozens of geese and swans croaked for handouts from bright spring families. I searched for the gateway from tourist park to walker's haven in the concrete walls of the highway. Finding the entrance, I ducked under Route 684, taking a barely used path straight up the steep hill. I humped up the slope quietly, planting my stick and treading on rocks. Reaching a flatter area, though not nearly at the top yet, the path wound through a stand of witch hazel. It exploded with a terrible crack and a deer sprang out, bouncing thirty yards away and staring at me. I stood there quietly. Why wasn't she running? And then I knew: a fawn probably lay in the dense thicket and she was leading me away. This was confirmed as I moved up the trail on an oblique angle towards her position. The trembling doe leaped another twenty yards and resumed her staring contest. I continued, waving to the frightened mother as the path veered away and up. I passed a run-down gazebo, over which an out-of-place, old-style diving wetsuit draped unceremoniously. The blue rubber had not yet rotted and must have been recently abandoned. I shrugged and continued up a rocky path, unsure of my position on the map, only knowing that if I continued skyward, I would reach my destination. A small rat snake hissed at me as I clambered over the rocks. I stopped and waited for the gray reptile to slide down into a dark gap and then proceeded, thrilled by this close encounter. The trail led me to a small peak, but not the chief one. Nevertheless, I plopped down on a flat shelf and ate a snack, watching a covey of hawks soaring over Meriden far below.

Studying the topographic map, I headed west, toward the afternoon sun, and after dipping into a gully, I ascended onto a previously developed area near the lookout tower on Castle Craig. A road gave evidence of the past here, when anyone could drive to this peak and climb the tower. But now, places like this and West Rock in New Haven have been closed to car traffic, leaving wonderful hill-roads for walkers and cyclists. I obviously approved.

I could see Talcott Mountain to the north and Sleeping Giant to the south, and wondered if I could find enough towers and peaks to map the entire state with my eyes. I considered all the other high points I had reached, all the bare ridges I had traversed, Mohawk Mountain, Mount Higby, Haystack Mountain, the list went on and on. I pondered the fact that many of these hikes had not been very difficult, yet the recollection remained strong. No doubt this was due to the sense of completion that a panoramic exclamation point gives.

Of course, hiking to the top of a mountain can be an accomplishment in its own right. One fine August day, having just returned from a seven-day hiking tour of England's Lake District and being in fairly good cardiovascular shape, I decided it was time I hiked up Bear Mountain, part of the Taconic Plateau, at an elevation of approximately 1800 feet, over a thousand above the surrounding valleys. This is one of four identified plateaus in our state, all formed of a more resistant granite and schist bedrock. Below are the marble lowlands that have eroded away in the acids of northeastern rainwater. Bear Mountain itself is 2316 feet tall, the highest peak in Connecticut. The shoulder of Mount Frissel, whose summit is in Massachusetts, is technically the highest point, but that didn't quite have the same romantic ring. So, I drove up Route 8 and west on 44 to Salisbury, where I found the Undermountain Trailhead and parked. Grasping my walking stick firmly, I shouldered my light pack and tramped up the hill. The rocky path became steep fairly quickly, but I was able to endure without stopping, keeping a slow but regular pace. I passed under the peak to the east, encountering no one, listening to the joyful August birds.

After a remarkably short interval, I reached the Massachusetts border and entered a grove of large hemlocks, where the spur ended at the white-blazed Appalachian Trail. After munching on an apple, I turned left and pushed steadily up the ledges and boulders to the remains of a crumbled monument on the peak. I climbed to the top and enjoyed the three-hundred-sixty degree view of the Riga Plateau and the Taconic Mountains: trees, trees, trees, as far as the eye could see, rolling ridges of rippling green. This was one of the prize views in Connecticut, quite frankly, mostly due to the fact that it is the only one involving significant mountains. I peered down at the Twin Lakes in Salisbury, where a year before I had unsuccessfully attempted to find and break into a lost, closed-up cave. North was our neighbor Massachusetts and I fancied I could see the gorge where I had once relaxed in the big trees of Bish-Bash Falls park. As I ate a small lunch, a family reached the summit from the other direction and then an entire class of Wesleyan University students. They were freshmen out for their introductory weekend. I had no idea Wesleyan used this unorthodox but brilliant method for initiating their students. I satisfied myself with unauthorized hikes in the company of my English students around the body of Sleeping Giant or out to Fayerweather Island in Bridgeport.

I chatted with the teacher and students for a while, and then tramped down the AT with views south and west into New York, where I glimpsed the storied peaks of the Catskills glimmering above the Hudson River Valley. Hitting the Undermountain Trail again, I trundled quickly down to my car. The book suggested four hours for this trip. I had taken two and a half, including at least forty-five minutes relaxing on the summit. I was sure I would never be in such great shape again. But I hoped that I would find another fine spectacle worthy of the effort.

Why are these views from high places so meaningful to the human psyche? People I know who have no love for the outdoors still treasure these rare, visionary moments. I have no real answer, only a story. Once I hiked up High Rock in Hamden after the loss of a friend, who was not much older than I was. He had wasted away with cancer, becoming a shell of himself, withdrawing into bitterness before dying. I felt old, like my life was also tipping into the void. As I walked up the path, a large black snake, at least five feet long, slithered across the trail and into deep, matted leaves. I found an unusually rounded boulder, like half an egg, and perched on top, reading Henry Miller's famous travelogue of Greece, *The Colossus of Maroussi*. A strangely diurnal bobcat bounded up the cliff edge, out of the brush, and stopped, astonished at my presence, then loped off into the woods.

As I sat on that wild island of stone in midst of civilized Connecticut, gazing over the small metropolis of New Haven, I meditated on my mortality, on inevitable change, on the power that loss has to destroy our will. The grim ghost of death had stalked me for the past few months, ruining my seemingly steadfast appreciation for nature. My steps had been weak and unenthusiastic lately. But now I stared down at the world I enjoyed and death seemed far away. The memory of my friend rustled the green backdrop of leaves, blessing rather than cursing me. I smiled, suddenly in love with everything around me, with the trees and the city, with the birds and the silence. I walked down the hill and into the summer of my life.

Chapter Eight

Heart of the Giant

F or many years I nearly always walked alone. I liked to ramble at my own pace, to stop when I want to, to explore. I liked the soothing quiet and the greater chance to see wildlife. But upon occasion I had enjoyed having companions on my treks through Connecticut. I got the chance to introduce them to the wild spaces between their houses and towns.

I suppose that's why I started taking my students at Quinnipiac University to the top of Sleeping Giant. I found that many students never crossed the street into one of our best state parks, despite the chin-cliff towering over the campus. This boggled my mind. So, without approval or pedagogy, I added a midterm in the fall and a final exam in the spring. The students in my freshman composition and literature classes would have to make it to the summit of the steep ridge. I did put in a provision – they could write a five page journal entry instead. And if someone attempted the climb and failed, credit would still be given. But my purpose held – to get them into the woods and skyward for the view. In the autumn I would take them up in October, when the leaves first burned into color. And in the spring, April, when fog crept around the new-minted banknote leaves.

Most of the students followed me up the steep, rocky path to the cliff of the giant's chin with reluctance. One girl described it as, "A million feet high and all rocks." They were compelled to encounter animals and plants up close, something that many had never done before. A mouse scuttled along the cliff edge once and quickly became an object of fascinated study. Crows attacked hawks in the wind-eddies above us. One of my students found a copperhead in the scree slopes at the base of the chin-cliff and another found a lost dog. Mostly, they found a sense of awe and possibly a new respect for the wilderness. At least, that's what I hope I provided with these risky jaunts into the Connecticut woods. Each time we went up I would picture one of them breaking an ankle or passing out from heat exhaustion, leading to an ambulance, an inquiry, and my dismissal. But no one was hurt, and nearly everyone enjoyed the view from the top, peering down at the tiny college below, listening to the distant clock tower bells. The miniature skyscraper cluster of New Haven seemed like a coastal fortress on the edge of the blue strip of the Sound. And when the Long Island residents realized they could see their homeland on the horizon, they never failed to utter oaths of amazement.

This process continued for a couple years, before it was kicked into high gear during one fall semester. A student from Hamden, Jeff, had been on the Giant even more times than I had, and knew a fascinating secret. When he first told me about the cave on the hill, I didn't fully believe him. His story seemed like half-remembered dreams of childhood, filled with the exaggerated heroics of the young. I thought perhaps there was a slight nook somewhere in the traprock ridges or perhaps that he was remembering some other place and transplanting it here to his hometown. I couldn't believe that I had hiked through Sleeping Giant State Park for years and been unaware of this mythic place.

So, as three of my students and I sweated up through one of the passes into the central plateau of this tiny hill kingdom, I wasn't really expecting to find anything. The ground was covered with the brown leaves of late fall and the thick trees hung with the last yellow soldiers. We scoured the bottom of the last cliff, the one before the crest of the hill, where the fabled castle looms above the trees. We caught a glimpse of that tower at one point along the trail, as Jerry told us the story about how he had gone up on Halloween night with a group of friends as a dare. I wished that we could still camp overnight there, as boy scouts had done for decades. Though perhaps I would have stayed there and never come down.

The hundred foot orange-gray bluffs spread out to our left. A dark opening that looked like a possible cave peeked from above the slope of boulders and scree left by the retreating glaciers. We clambered up. The opening went in only a few feet. Another one dipped into the earth, but was blocked by a huge boulder.

"Nope. Maybe further along." Jeff pushed along the edge of the cliff with Jerry. Russ and I climbed back down and followed along the trail for about a quarter mile.

"I don't really think there's a cave up there." I told Russ. He nodded.

"Here it is!" Jeff shouted.

"No way." We pushed up the mossy boulder field. "Watch out for snakes." I laughed, half-serious.

Jeff was standing on a tall rock at the mouth of what looked like a cave. I set down my pack and switched places with him. A crevasse ran straight into the cliff, into darkness. A real cave. A rarity! Simply created by the way the rock cracked and fell when glaciers ripped through here millennia ago. No water or force dug this cave. It was simply there.

After stashing our equipment in a hole, we followed Jeff slowly up over the doorwarden boulder and down into the dark crack. About twenty feet in, the passage ended, and a seventy-five-degree slope from the left dropped into nothing. Our flashlights waved around the rock faces, searching for a hold.

"Could someone else go first?" Jeff pulled himself back from the edge slowly.

Everyone paused. "Sure," I said. As we slid past each other in the tight passage, I sensed fear in Jeff's eyes. As I looked down into the dark, I felt it, too. The drop didn't look that far, but I wasn't sure about the slick, smooth, near-ninety degree angle of the walls. And the log propped on the opposite wall to assist climbers looked old and rotten. I just wasn't sure.

"Maybe we should come back with a rope."

The four of us considered and voted that this was probably the best option. Normally, I might have forged ahead, but this was not something I really wanted to take a risk with. I could lose my job if one of my companions was hurt. Fear held me back. I had never done anything quite like this before.

Still, the next day I went to Trailblazer in downtown New Haven and purchased a climbing rope. I bought their cheapest one, for a hundred dollars, telling the Birkenstocked salesgirl that I only wanted it for "top-rope" climbing. The whole time in the store I could hear Samwise Gamgee from *The Lord of the Rings* saying, "If only we had some rope, Mr. Frodo!"[1] Fifty meters long, neon yellow and black, and coiled on my living room floor, it took on an impressive, epic quality. I took an hour and taught myself how to tie a climbers knot, making sure that I could do it in the dark time and time again. This may seem like a simple, almost comical reaction, but doing something new and unknown should always produce these mixed feelings of fear and excitement.

I also did a little research and found out that the cave had a long and storied history going back hundreds of years. Tours had been given during the 1800s, when the Giant had human inhabitants perched in cabins on the glaciated ridges. Someone had gotten stuck and the private tours had shut down. Then, in the 1890s, two boys had come up to see the cave and instead found a dead body at the entrance. One of the famous Barnum family had committed suicide by jumping off the top cliff and landing near the entrance to what was now called "Dead Man's Cave."

Most of the larger caves in Connecticut are now closed. Bashful Lady Cave in far northwest Salisbury, formed in the marble lowlands, is actually the longest cave in New England, but cannot be entered by the casual spelunker today. Bad conditions and vandalism have put an end to the age of caves in Connecticut, and now only die-hard cavers sneak over fences onto private properties to find the openings to lower worlds.

And now here I was considering going into this cave with my students. Was I crazy? Probably. But even as visions of lawsuits filled my head, I knew that this descent into the earth would make an impression on them. They would remember this unique experience for the rest of their lives, wriggling through a tunnel in the dark with their English professor, accomplishing something they perhaps didn't feel was possible.

I certainly wasn't afraid anyone was going to be seriously wounded. But even a minor injury could not only have serious consequences for me, but for the cave itself. Cemented up? Blocked off by court order? Surely the park rangers knew about this place? Wouldn't they have done that long ago? I suppose it only takes one accident.

Jeff, Jerry, Russ, and I returned the next Friday, with my new rope and more flashlights. Jeff had admitted to the rest of us that he was deathly afraid of spiders, and I hoped we wouldn't find the place crawling with them. Or snakes. I hadn't smelled the usual musk of other animals or seen droppings the last time we came up, so I was fairly sure we wouldn't run into anything larger. Jeff had seen two particularly large and hairy spiders when he was peering over the edge last week, which is why he balked at going down. I had desisted for a more subtle reason.

At the entrance, I found a suitable rock formation and tied the rope perfectly. Jeff commented on the knot and I mock-snorted. "Some eagle scout you are!"

"Knots weren't my strong point." He shrugged, laughing.

I tested the climber's knot and then carried the loop with me into the wedge of the first passage. The others followed. At the lip of the drop, I tossed the coil into the darkness. "All right."

"Put your foot on that log." Jeff pointed past my shoulder at the opposite wall.

"Right." I put my flashlight in my pocket and gingerly stretched my left leg to the wood, while Jeff and Jerry used their flashlights to maximum effect. My left hand clutched the slippery wall. As I got my balance between the ledge and log, I could see a ledge that had been hidden until now, complete with an ancient candle. I slid my left foot down the log and reached the ledge. "No problem!" I glanced back at my students. My right foot swung off the drop and to the new source of support. I was easily able to slide myself down the steep wall and put a foot on a rock near the floor.

The new passage doubled back below and parallel to the first one. However, the dank corridor was much smaller and continued to narrow until it reached a black hole in the stone. Ignoring that for the moment, I pulled out my lighter and lit the candle. Then, I helped Jeff find the secret ledge and we slid down this second channel one by one. As I was pushed towards the black hole, I found another candle in a niche and lit it. Then, I pointed my flash into the hole. The floor of the cave below looked far. This would be the real challenge.

"This is a bit scary, guys."

"No kidding."

"No, I mean this just drops off into nothing."

I threw the glowing coil of rope down and it hit the floor. Maybe it wasn't that far. I couldn't see enough and I was going to have to pocket the flashlight again. Damn. All right. I reached out and held onto the ledge to my right and put my left hand forward. I realized I couldn't get my feet down this way, because the ceiling was preventing me from moving up. So, I had to push back. "Hold on, guys, I have to switch." I worked myself around and put my feet on the log instead. Then, it was a matter of dipping myself into the unknown. I lowered myself into the spidery darkness. My feet touched a pointed piece of stone. I twisted my arms down, balancing on the only wall near enough. Then I stepped off this lucky rock and onto the floor below. I immediately pulled the flashlight out of my pocket and searched the dense darkness. The cave was the size of a small room, with a spearhead of rock on the roof dividing it into two.

I helped my students down one by one, then lit a candle and set it on a small rock. The four of us crouched in the empty space inside the hill, looking around in wonder. Spray-paint from years past tattooed the walls. Who knows how many explorers, children, and madmen have delved into this niche in the mountain? But it was not the unknown that brought us here. The discoveries we were here to make were of another sort.

At the far end a channel proceeded up and to the right. I crawled up along the slippery rock and peered into another room, about the size of a large closet. All of a sudden, Jerry pushed all of us ahead with a slight scream. "What is that?!" I slipped down and shone my flashlight. A tiny brown bat, asleep on the wall. "Just a bat, guys." After they calmed down, we flipped the flashlights off and sat in the dark. Creepy. A tight passage dove under the main chamber, but none of us had any desire to slip along this tiny crevice. Perhaps another day.

Before we ascended, I took a last look around. I knew that this was a classroom I could really teach in. I knew I would take students here again and again. A month later I started this process. Jeff and I went back, taking three girls from the class with us. They passed with flying colors, clambering in and out without a problem. This became a ritual every year, taking first-year students to this magic place. They would take others there, opening this hidden world to friends and classmates. One semester I took nearly fifty students to Dead Man's Cave, sometimes going twice a weekend, never tiring of the process or the results. I left a small, white rock in a secret place there, a tiny memento of the lesson learned. Every time a group of students walked back from the cave, chatting excitedly about the experience, pride filled my heart. Back in the parking lot, they always thanked me and, as I drove home each time, I knew that I had made a difference. And that's probably the only reason to leave the woods in the first place.

Chapter Nine

Deliberation and Accident

Ipicked the particular apartment I lived in during those early years for a particular reason: the large window in my living room looked directly into the forest. I huddled in a hobbit-hole, half buried in a hill, on the lowest level of a condo complex. On days when the weather did not cooperate with my desire to walk, I sat in my easy chair, sipped tea, and watched television like anyone else. But my eyes drifted to that window, searching for cardinals and robins in the wetland trees, watching squirrels run along the highway of the fencetop. Beyond that fence was a jungle, which choked the wooden bars. Sometimes, I'd step onto my porch to listen to the wind in the treetops or catch the last rays of sunlight that streamed into my tiny world every clear day. I tested the grass, which led everywhere...grass that led to a path, that led to a greenway, that led... The temperate jungle beyond called me. "Walk," it said. "Explore."

Unlike real explorers, however, I didn't often get lost. I usually prepared maps carefully and took my time, intent on a definite goal. Some of my more fly-by-night friends criticized me for this, but forethought can make for a smoother and more enjoyable experience. I trembled at the idea of missing some important landmark or wasting precious time backtracking. Getting lost seemed to be a luxury for those people who preferred to remain blissfully unaware and had unlimited free time. And so I never really got lost on my walks in Connecticut until one fine summer day in the Cockaponset State Forest near the town of Deep River, with my first Connecticut friend.

Ironically, this first friend, Chris, was not from Connecticut at all. He was a transplant like me, coming from New Hampshire and before that Oregon. His knowledge of the outdoors derived partly from time working there for the National Forest Service, and he taught me a lot on our forays into hiking. He was a voracious eater, a constant runner, and a celebrated English Education teacher. His wife, Alison, and his beautiful female Belgian Shepherd, Harpo, sometimes joined us on these treks. But at first I was hesitant to expand my circle past one friend. I had grown quite used to my solitude.

Driving in to the trailhead, Chris and I passed the inland beachgoers who were soaking up the sun on the shore of the lake. But we were not here for lazing on the sand, we were here to hike about eight miles into the surprisingly empty quarter between the Connecticut River and New Haven. Immediately, I made a wrong turn in the jumble of temporary paths and lost the proper trail. But Chris forged ahead, unfazed by the lack of blazes. He told me stories of his days with the forest service as we wandered on ancient logging roads and horse trails, one of which finally dead-ended at private land. Backtracking, I marveled at the complexity of this trail system, none of which was on the map. How many more areas like this was I missing by staying on the blazed trails?

An hour and a half later we found the blue trail, which ran parallel to the perfectly good path we had taken out of the Cockaponset labyrinth. Continuing, we discovered a miniature toad near a five-foot high property wall in excellent condition. Just there we met a couple missing a brown Labrador named Buck. "He's always running off like this, but we can't find him at all this time," the tie-dyed man told us. "We'll keep our eyes open," Chris assured them. We stopped at a junction marked "6" and realized that we'd only came a few miles on the planned route, though far more than that as the wolf runs. As we sat there, contemplating how we had gone astray, Buck the brown lab came whuffling down a hill and approached us, tail wagging. Chris rigged a leash out of his jacket, fed Buck jerky and water, and whistled for the couple. A family wandered by and miraculously had just found a rope, which promptly replaced the jacket. "How lucky!" the mother of the family exclaimed.

Then, our decision made for us by necessity, we headed back towards the trailhead. Just then the owner ran breathlessly up the trail, having heard our far-away whistling. "Thank you so much," he gasped. "Keep the rope," Chris chuckled. As our new friend Buck trotted along next to his master, he looked decidedly smug. He had an adventure, probably better than ours, all by getting himself lost.

I briefly thought about retracing and continuing, attempting to stick to my original plan, but instead we walked contemplatively back along the lakeside. Small fishing boats puttered about in the tiny coves. Suddenly, two children popped out of the brush, one scared little boy eyeing us with apprehension. His older brother reassured him, "They're just hikers. You're just hikers, right?" I was tempted to say, "No!" and give them a fun and scary adventure of their own, but didn't. Who knows if their parents would have taken it as well as they would have. Adults have often forgotten the lure of the unknown that every day of childhood brings. And that is what was lost when I planned out my hikes too carefully…the sense of adventure, the mapping of the unknown, the happy accidents of experience.

With this lesson in mind, I decided to try something new one day at the Larsen Nature Sanctuary. Instead of marking my goal as a distance to be traversed or a finish line to reach, I decided my goal would be to see wildlife, taking a random route through the maze of trails. I was there for a "slow walk," treading softly, staying silent. I brought no walking stick, wanting both hands free for my binoculars.

A corridor of red maples, eastern hemlock, Norway spruce, and yellow birch led me into a wonderland. Step by step I crept through the September woods, to where a black-tailed young stag browsed. We stared at each other for ten minutes until he moved deeper into the forest.

I tried defocusing my eyes to catch movement, letting my feet see the ground ahead. It worked and I saw a doe chewing twigs and leaves. Her black muzzle pointed to me, but her pink ears swiveled to catch sound from other directions. The trees swayed in the wind and a golden beam of sunlight burnished her with a chestnut-orange hue. I stayed there for longer than I usually would, mind-melding with her, then slow-walked past, looking in another direction to ease her mind.

I practiced not snapping twigs with my usually clumsy feet. I passed
one of the two-hundred-year-old stone walls that crisscrossed the property and entered a brilliant sunlit meadow, full of yellow honeysuckle
and goldenrod. Insects chattered and hummed. I explored a small side
trail and found a horse farm packed with brown and white stallions and
mares. Squirrels prattled at me, giant blue dragonflies spun through the
air, and a hawk wheeled above the meadow. Details! I always told my students to pay attention to them and now I was learning the same lesson. I
sniffed out faint deer trails, bird houses on poles, and thickets full of bird
life. They startled and flew out as I passed.

Then, due to a momentary lapse of attention, I missed four deer
flanking the path. With a mighty snort the leader commanded the others
off into the forest. I had to be more careful. One brave young stag stayed
by the path and I watched him for a while. New horns sprouted from the
young deer's skull and he eyed me uncertainly. Then, an entire herd appeared along a long stone wall. I stayed for about half an hour, then continued down a long boardwalk, carefully avoiding dried leaves and twigs.

As I wandered through the sanctuary, I reached a wild pond, covered
in a thin layer of green slime. I studied a small red dragonfly, noting yellow at the base of its wings, tiny spots, and a large black head. Wood duck
boxes poked out of the pond and a few of their inhabitants dipped wet
bills into the marshy weeds. Then, in another meadow, another deer ran
past me. These nature sanctuaries weren't exactly wild places, but they
certainly were full of wild life! I headed down a country lane flanked by
stone walls and ferns, the remnants of an ancient town road, crossing a
pipeline corridor and thinking of how tempting it would be to follow
these around the state on an alternate web.

A flicker of movement to my right. I scanned the woods. Six wild
turkeys! I studied them with my binoculars until they moved behind a
hillock. Earlier, I had decided not to go off-trail in this nature sanctuary, but fate had other plans, allowing the path to disappear like smoke.
Something, another deer no doubt, bounded through the cover far to my
left. And there were those turkeys! We had taken different routes and
met in a huge glade split by one of the omnipresent stone walls. They
fled into the brush and I found the trail at the crumbling foundation
of a house. Frogs splashed into creeks at my approach, no matter how
stealthy I tried to be. Thick beech trees ruled this rare climax forest, the

carvings of lovers expanding slowly in their elephantine bark.

I found a stone wall slightly off the path, sat down, and ate a lunch of sardines, chocolate, and apples. Morel mushrooms sprouted around me. I had brought a book to read, but sometimes nature is all you need to study. A chipmunk on the wall, a squirrel in the ferns, a spiderweb high in an oak tree…these were my pages and, better yet, ones I had found by accident.

After these experiences, I made getting lost on purpose one of my rituals. On a late October day I traveled up a road that a century ago was called the "Backbone Route to the North" in New Haven County. I hiked a mile or so in from a quiet suburban development on the Quinnipiac Trail. Hitting a long, grassy pipeline corridor, I turned left and up a short rise. At the top I was greeted with a grassy slope down into Cheshire with the best view of Meriden's mighty Hanging Hills I'd ever had. Not satisfied with this diversion, I continued on the blue-trail for a bit, then shot off across a swamp, crossed the corridor again, and found a fascinating "tor" much like the ones in the moorlands of England. Twisted and cracked rock formations topped this small hill, and I imagined that hundreds of years ago, when this land was denuded of trees, the settlers felt right at home.

I was not worried about getting too far off-track, knowing that a road or house was probably right around the corner. Getting lost in the wilderness of Alaska can be a deadly experience. But here in Connecticut it is a luxury we can afford. So, I lazed on that rocky prominence and boiled water for hot chocolate with my stove. I cracked open my usual tin of sardines and a hazelnut wafer bar. Wind in the trees was the only sound in this hidden corner of the Connecticut suburbs. Sipping the last of my chocolate, I reached into my pack for a notebook when a shadow moved in the trees below. I froze and stared in the forest. A dog? But dogs made more noise. And that loping trot looked familiar…a coyote. A primal thrill went through me. My first Connecticut coyote. I had seen coyotes out west, but here! Later, I talked to a woman who lived in the nearby development and she confirmed my sighting. "We can hear them howling at night," she told me.

Excited by the encounter, I moved off, uncertain how to find the blue trail again. I knew a coyote couldn't hurt me, but I remained jumpy as I searched for the path, picking my way through poison ivy patches and downed tree limbs. Crash! Two deer suddenly burst from a thicket and I started, instincts kicking in, suddenly part of the great theater of the wilderness, brought there by blind accident, but full of bright purpose. Trembling, I moved onwards, searching for the way. Who knows what adventures awaited me, now that I had found the courage to lose myself here in the gaps between the suburbs.

Chapter Ten

On Returning

Returning to a place you once had an experience is a chancy prospect. Perhaps you are hoping for a repeat of an earlier encounter, an improved mental state, or maybe just better weather. Usually what you get is a disappointment, either slight or great. Over the years I have often complained about the negative ramifications of these returns, and have even preached against them to students and friends. But as usual, the forests of Connecticut had surprises hidden amongst the mushrooms and ferns.

The trail up Candlewood Mountain had been one of the first I tried in Connecticut. I had gone with that college girlfriend before things went downhill with her. And so, Candlewood had a particular place in my heart, although it was also a site of failure. After wasting time searching for the parking lot, my ex-girlfriend and I had hiked up Pine Knob, clambering up the glacier-abandoned rocks of the corkscrew to the secondary peak of the mountain. But time was against us, and we weren't sure how far it was to the main peak. So, frustrated, we turned around and left it for another day, rushing back to New Haven to keep an appointment. In my mind it was always unfinished business.

So, uncertain, I walked it again five years later. I went with the long-

haired, often-bearded Chris, who was becoming a regular hiking part-
ner. We drove to the far-off trailhead struggling up Route 7 north of
Danbury, which was blocked by hordes of summer tourists. After the
same problem finding the trailhead that I had previously, we entered the
narrow passage of woodlands. A large dog barked and ran after us a little
way. Chris picked up a suitable walking stick and used it for a while, but
when throwing the large branch on a rock shelf, the top portion broke
off. Inside a bright green mold and a hibernating carpenter bee surprised
and baffled us.

The two of us slid over long rock slides, slick with recent rain, glimps-
ing a strange neon-orange lizard that I looked up later, identifying it as a
red eft. The brown trails sprouted different species of mushrooms with
wide, flat red tops and small spherical white tops. We explored a small
cave in a jumble of boulders, then ate lunch on a log at the top of a cliff
overlooking the Housatonic Valley. The far-off cheers of a football game
wafted up through the air. At the very top of Candlewood Mountain
someone had erected an eight-foot cross, secured by climbing ropes, surrounded by a small chapel area of rocks. We looped around an old fire
road, now covered in a gentle grass sheet, then rambled back to the car.

On our way out, we stopped at the White Silo Winery and sampled
several fruit wines. The vineyard had just been featured on National Public Radio and the employees were in high spirits. The two elderly ladies
working there regaled us with all the places in the area to get gourmet
food, including a chocolatier in Kent and a pork farm in New Milford.
We drank full glasses of cool sangria and enjoyed the cellar breeze of the
winery and the pastoral paintings on the walls.

Chris and I had walked further, had spent more time, had a fuller
and richer experience. I overwrote my earlier hike with a greater one,
replacing failure with success. That is an easy way to look at return posi-
tively, though. What about a previously triumphant hike? What reason
is there to return to the site of a victory?

One overcast autumn day, a girl named Jordan and I walked down
the old woods trail at Wadsworth Falls State Park. I made small talk,
getting to know this new friend. We passed our impressive state flower, a
gigantic mountain laurel bush, and then dipped down a trail to the first
waterfall. A middle-aged couple went by us at a jog, speaking in some
Slavic language. I thought back to my time on this trail with that long-

lost ex-girlfriend many years ago. It had been one of the last places I explored with her in our small state, and had felt like quite an accomplishment. My world had changed so much in that time. These trails felt short now, easy and small. When I first explored here I was out of shape and did not have the long years of walking under my belt. Jordan and I barely knew each other, perhaps at the beginning of a friendship, while that other relationship had been nearing an end.

My new friend and I gazed at the rushing water, then walked briskly to the next waterfall, which poured over a huge ledge in a mini-Niagara. The last time I was here, the glistening flow was clearly much reduced. And I felt that I, too, was flowing faster and deeper now. Jordan and I walked back, spotting a small brown frog and a three-foot Eastern Ribbon Snake. We made a loop down into a gorge, where we tried to worm through an old water pump station. But the concrete gaps had been blocked off—more changes.

We left, and I was glad I hadn't come back alone, but felt like my walks needed something more now. I had moved to another stage, another level of goals for my walks. Still, this afternoon had not been a disappointment, it had simply been different, a beginning rather than an ending, an unsure colloquy rather than the comfortable dialogue of two old friends. When we change, everything around us changes. And thus, two hikes are never really the same.

But my real lesson about return came more recently, on a hike through a section of Connecticut's woodlands that had become commonplace and rote, Naugatuck State Forest and Brooksvale Park. I had taken these trails with groups of students, Ryan and Jenifer, and my ex. Once, I took a girl named Lindsey into this park, pointing out the stony remnants of a past age. We explored off the trail and found a spot in the center of a quiet wood. There we talked, discussing future possibilities, but then hurried back to my car, as she had to call her boyfriend. She moved to New Jersey and I never saw her again.

Now I was here once more. Why? Because it was a good example of the colonial ruins that dotted our state. It was an easy walk. It was close to my apartment. It was comfortable. This time I took two new acquaintances, Michelle and Melissa. The autumn before I had taken them to the cave on Sleeping Giant. That, too, had sadly become old hat, something I took students to every fall and spring, something that had lost its subtle magic. The three of us sat in the cool, dry heart of the Giant and told stories, losing track of time. As we sauntered down the hill, I smiled at their exuberance and effortless hiking skills. "That was fantastic!" Michelle gushed, and all the joy of sharing the forests came back to me, all the miraculous wonders of exploration.

The three of us took the same meandering trail I had always taken, which led to the heart of the old hill town. But after I showed them the well-preserved roads and walls, we took a trail I never had ventured on before. We found two ruined piles of stones that we ascertained were ovens, and then passed through a high pine forest with views of the looming Mount Sanford. I showed them how to collect birch bark to use for lighting fires. We stopped by a flooded field and watched two pairs of ducks paddle and dive. The layers of personal experience matched the layers of history on the stone-walled, ancient roads. Sitting on a log, they questioned me about my own history, and I regaled them with stories of other hikes and times. "You should have children to share all this with," Michelle told me, "Or a wife." I nodded solemnly, bowing to her fresh prophetic wisdom, but unaware of the returning I would one day do, and the person I would do it with, still unseen at that time, a whisper of wind in the purpling beech trees.

The entire afternoon passed as we sat there in the center of those beneficent, quiet woodlands. Occasionally, we heard other visitors, a cyclist, a family, but never saw them. Finally, at some hidden signal, we stood up and slowly made our way back. "My boyfriend and I broke up last night," Melissa confessed as we watched the peacocks in their nature center cages near the car. Shocked, I tried to comfort her, but she told me, "Today has really helped get my mind off it." I never would have guessed, and blessed her for allowing the dreamlike day to proceed without this harsh reality.

I learned my greatest lesson about following old trails that day. Something about these two companions allowed me to open up, to share, to look at things in a new way, through their clear, untarnished eyes. And what's more, I wanted to walk with them; my solitary rambles had needed something, something I hadn't quite realized until then. The people we hike with are what really matters, and return is just another word for restoration.

Chapter Eleven

Walking the Streams

After a short loop walk along a ridge with views of both the noble Catskills and the green, rounded Litchfield Hills, I returned to the campsite by the river. My tent balanced carefully on a sandy promontory, surrounded on three sides by water. Black birch and maple trees rose around the small but well-situated site at the heart of some of the greatest hiking in Connecticut. I had already spotted a small lizard, chipmunks, a toad, a garter snake that turned to look at me with cold eyes, and several groups of friendly dayhikers. I was here for more than hiking, though. I had come to Macedonia Brook State Park to fish for brook trout, to enjoy the slow evening time of feeding.

Above the campsite on the other side of the road perched an older road, now grassy, curved, and soft. A stone wall held in the path like a dam embracing a flood. Why was it abandoned? The way seemed perfectly sound. But I shouldn't complain. It now made the ideal walker's road, and as I leisurely fished the river I saw dozens of late afternoon couples and families taking advantage of this green gift. Normally, I would have joined them, but today I walked the stream instead.

I don't remember who suggested fly-fishing, my father or me. He lived in Pennsylvania, but visited Connecticut often on business. Once, we walked from the lot at Chatfield Hollow to the "Indian Caves," one of a hundred such sites across the state. Archaeological evidence apparently proves that in pre-Colonial times Indians used the valley for hunting and fishing and the number of items discovered in the vicinity of Indian Council Caves suggest that Native Americans held tribal gatherings there. However, common belief is that these were Indian "homes," a ridiculous prejudice. I'm sure no self-respecting Native American would have made a home here in any of these minor holes in the Connecticut cliffs, unless they had been forced to by the incursions of the Europeans. Perhaps they used them when on walkabouts and on hunting trips, but not as permanent homes. Fellow moderns did use them, however; fire rings and beer cans always litter them. My father and I walked around the cliff and clambered up the trail to the top, where we could look down through the chimney and at the sides of the hollow.

My father was not much of a hiker, though. Our real adventures began on the rivers, which he had loved since he was a child. And so, for my birthday one year he gave me all his old gear, along with a book on the basics. I had fished in my own childhood, but hadn't cast a line in about fifteen years. And I had never used a fly rod, never put on waders and headed down a stream to hunt for trout. Which is exactly what my father began to teach me: how to wade, to cast, and to perform all the little functions that make a successful angler. Later, when we began catching trout, he taught me how to clean a fish and how to bake it in my stove.

Connecticut stocks its rivers with over a half million trout and a couple thousand salmon. More than four-thousand of its six-thousand five-hundred and eighty seven miles of rivers and streams have wild trout, as well. This is an astonishing fact, especially considering our small acreage compared to, say our neighbor to the west. On my hikes through the state, I inevitably crossed fishable streams, with angling signs and the occasional lone fisherman, sitting patiently on a stump or wading through the river like a heron. We have some great fishing, and the most wonderful thing is how close all of it is. Where I grew up in Pennsylvania, the fishable streams and rivers were long drives apart. Here, I could nearly hop from one to another, fishing my way across the state, and don't think I haven't considered that option.

On that marvelous first day of my Connecticut fishing experience, my father and I arrived at 6:00 a.m. after many others were already stationed on the picturesque Mill River in Hamden. Leaf-litter and branches choked the brook trails. Avoiding them, we began to wade the stream. Suddenly, a new and electrifying world opened to me. Instead of trail, or greenway, or haunted back road, I was walking a new corridor, full of merry sights and sounds. Fish appeared beneath my feet, swimming frantically for cover. Restless, spring birds swept back and forth from bank to bank. Along that one short stretch of the Mill under the looming head of the Sleeping Giant, I saw a hawk dive at a duck, an osprey catch a fish, a snapper turtle and water snake wriggle past my legs, and legions of trout waiting solemnly in deep, clear pools. And I met dozens of fishermen, all friendly and inquisitive. "What fly are you using?" "How many today?" "Water's too low, ain't?" My father and I drank morning coffee together, shared stories of outdoor experiences, and reveled in our fish.

At Macedonia Brook years later, I lit a small fire to roast potatoes. While they warmed, I cooked pasta and boiled lemon tea. Wind whispered through the tall trees around the camp, nestled in the hanging brook valley. Hills rose on all sides. The brook curved and curled around boulders and logs. Dragonflies flitted around the campsite – green, blue, brown, and black. A few tried for my small green fly, but changed their minds at the last second, as unfortunately did the fingerling native brook trout. I saw nothing over five inches, but perhaps they just knew better and hid. My tiny army-style tent had not been used in eight years, too small to comfortably fit two. But for this lonely fishing expedition it was sadly perfect.

I planned on heading to the mighty Housatonic River the next morning, where my dad and I had our most successful expedition ever. I actually convinced him to camp with me at Housatonic Meadows State Park, meeting there like two gypsies. Then, we walked the river, step by step, catching trout and smallmouth bass. The warm August water made waders unnecessary, my sandals gripping the slippery underwater rocks. Eager birds dove in the canyon, catching mosquitoes and flies in the evening air. Other fishermen remained sedentary, standing and casting, switching flies with frustration. We explored forward and backward, side to side, wandering the stream. The waist-deep water rushed by. That day I knew for sure I had found a new perspective and terrain to explore. This walking was different, allowing for a slower and more precise experience. I could feel every step, examine every overhanging tree, and live every moment with absolute care.

After a night in front of a roaring fire, we drove to nearby Kent Falls State Park. It was not a walker's paradise, though the staircase up the nine-waterfall cascade made for an amazing quarter mile. I scaled it while my father sat on the rock ledges by the bottom-most pool and fly-fished. He caught seven native brook trout in only half an hour, letting a nymph drift with the water over the falls, where the unsuspecting fish gulped it down. Then, he drove me back to the trailhead for the classic Lion's Head hike and left for home in Pennsylvania, happy with his impressive catch. More than the fish for me, though, was time spent walking the stream. And somehow, more than that was time spent with my father doing it. Although I often chased the eternally slippery quarry from pool to pool on my own, having my father there made it greater.

All these memories were with me as I relaxed by that June fire, the smell of citronella and woodsmoke mingling pleasantly in the summer air. The constant gurgle of the brook comforted and surrounded me. Ferns and flowers encircled the sandy area. A park ranger came and talked to me briefly, handing me a car permit. "You've got the luxury suite here!" I knew it. The evening deepened and clouds covered the sky. Forecast for tomorrow was rain. Bah! If I stopped walking every time rain became imminent, I would never get anything accomplished.

The sound of the stream took me back again, to earlier that spring when the circle became complete. On the first day of fishing season, my brother joined my father and me at the usual 6:00 a.m. and parked under the shadow of Sleeping Giant by the Mill River, named for the corn mill installed by the founders of New Haven centuries earlier. Like my father, my brother was not exactly a walker, but he was here to share this experience. The dark, muddy river rushed along, higher than I had ever seen it. I tried to fish the upper section, but the murky water splashed into my hip boots. So, I walked along the old quarry road, past where I could see my father teaching my brother how to cast a fly properly, and found a miraculously unfished section of stream. I immediately snared a nice trout. Showing my family this abnormally productive stretch of stream, which no other angler had found yet, I smiled at their enthusiasm. My brother hooked his first fish in twenty years. I caught another and my father quickly captured his limit. In the shadowless afternoon, we attempted to fish the gorgeous Farmington River, with its white, dinosaur egg boulders and steep canyon walls, but it was running about a foot too high and we caught only spring air. That didn't matter. I was following the path of Connecticut's shining rivers with my family, and if this was the only way I could get them into the forest with me, then so be it.

We fished the Quinnipiac Gorge in Cheshire, where I caught an ancient trout, so heavy that I accidentally dropped it back into the cool brown stream. We fished the Salmon River near Colchester, under the Comstock covered bridge, where my father and I walked up the gorge and down the stream, feeling every inch of the stony bottom imprinted on our footsoles. I fought a huge trout for ten minutes before landing it, then triumphantly baked it for lunch in butter and lemon, enjoying every delicate morsel of my victory. And when my brother moved to Springfield, MA, we fished the deep-running Scantic River northeast of Hartford, catching browns and rainbows, meeting in the middle like all families must do.

I caught nothing that summer evening on the solemn Macedonia Brook. The fire died, the night closed in, and I slept. The next morning thunderstorms blew in, ruining my plans for another morning of fishing, in spite of my tough attitude the night before. But none of that mattered. I vowed to bring my family to that brook next time, promised to ramble even farther along that tiny, loitering stream, and maybe even get them to stroll the old grassy road with me. Trout were not the only reason I made my slow, unhurried way along the little rivers and streams of green Connecticut.

Chapter Twelve

Second Campaign Across Connecticut

Ryan and I parked at an intersection off of Route 179 in East Hartland, above the huge reservoir that drowned old farmlands under forty feet of water. We girded on our backpacks and crossed the road into the cool October forest. The leaves had rusted to burnt umber and drifted lazily around our heads. The old, rock-strewn tote road had been transformed into a stream by recent rains. But it opened up into a beautifully dry, yellow lane, flanked by stone walls. We crunched along and then veered off to the "Indian Council Caves," simply a jumble of rocks where artifacts had been found. We scoffed at the pseudoscience and myth behind these names and then struggled up some cliffs, which gave us brief views. I let my long-time Pennsylvania friend lead, but had to pull him back when he took the wrong fork at several junctions. We were hiking the section I should have completed on that long-ago attempt to cross the state. I felt ambivalent about this, but considered it necessary for some part of my soul.

We crossed long, luminous meadows above a beaver-dammed stream. Browning autumn ferns brushed our feet. More logging roads appeared, recently used by state forest agents, and we got lost briefly, then found the hidden blue trail sneaking off into some hemlocks to our right.

Huge oak trees, perhaps two-hundred years old, occasionally loomed
over the trail, often splitting into multiple trunks due to long-past fires
and diseases. We continued up steady rises, ascending the highest point
in the area, which unfortunately had no view. But after a short rest and
a snack, Ryan began walking down the trail and stepped directly over a
porcupine without noticing it. I called him back and we studied it for a
while. The animal appeared dead, not moving a muscle even when prod-
ded gently. But it had not decayed and unless it had died within the hour,
it was playing possum, so to speak. We left it alone and continued down
the hill, across crumbling stone property boundaries, and reached Route
20. We crossed it and dove back into the red-brown woods. After another brief snack, we reached a quiet back road, crossed it, and ascended
a hill to a look-out, which had probably been excellent years ago, but the
venerable trees had grown too high. While we peered at the Barkham-
sted Reservoir, a very large but unseen animal moved around in the forest
below. Ryan scanned the trees nervously for a bear.

Nevertheless, we continued along the blue blazes, descending and
ascending a few ravines until we reached a pleasant open area by a stream,
with a long, low log to sit on. We took off our packs, boiled tea with
my Primus, and cooked turkey chili. After a wonderful meal and a chat
under the falling leaves, we decided to head back. When we reached
the road, a black squirrel scooted across it in front of us. I had never
seen one of these rare animals and always thought that they were dark
gray, but this one was like a tiny piece of night. We took Route 20 and
struggled up it, feeling the breeze of passing trucks and weekend drivers.
We tramped for three miles up and down the macadam slopes until we
reached the car, tired but somehow exhilarated by our effort and experience.

We had talked only briefly of my failed hike that far-off, inauspicious, rainy May. But this occasion had sealed it, brought back the idea.
I knew I couldn't or wouldn't want to try the same route. So, I searched
the internet, maps, and guidebooks, trying to find a better route across
the state. But I failed, over and over. There simply weren't enough state
parks or motels or hotels or bed and breakfasts, at least in the right places
for a north-south hike, a fact that somewhat baffled me. Then, I checked
out the private campgrounds, which had failed to appear in the central
part of the state. But in the eastern section, they scattered across the hol-

low landscape like gold dust. Sure, there were still a few long sections of campless area, but I finally had hope. What's more, I realized I must not try it alone this time. Knowing he had the strength within him to finish what he started, I invited Ryan and after a struggle to find vacation time he accepted, leaving Jenifer and their pet rabbit at home.

And so it was that the loyal Chris drove us to the marina just north of I-95 on Route 156 one sunny day in May. I had wanted to start at Selden's Neck, the largest island in the Connecticut River, the true starting point of the landscape, but various factors made this impossible. Still, the bridge towered above us, Long Island Sound glimmered in the distance, and boats were being scrubbed and polished for the upcoming summer. After pictures and farewells, Ryan and I began our walk through Old Lyme. Almost immediately, we were forced to stop to adjust and repack Ryan's bag. After quite a bit of disorder, our walking sticks pounded once again on the busy road. We received two honks, a wave, and a nod from the passing travelers. An old man with a beautiful horse farm assured us, "that'll keep you fit," when we told him our plans. A woman in a Range Rover stopped and yelled, "You guys been goin' a long way. I passed you three times today!"

We set a slow pace, trying to avoid the problems I faced before. As we walked, we spoke of religion, hobbies, and past hikes. Finally we entered the town of Lyme, the place where the eponymously named disease was discovered. A good spot for lunch appeared under a huge tree by an old church. We could have eaten lunch inside, but instead relaxed under the spreading oak, taking our faith from the beautiful world. Laying back on the soft grassy hillside, we devoured meat, cheese, and chocolate, a real mountaineer's lunch. Old-fashioned fire trucks from the Lyme station screamed past. Sated, we continued, passing the quaint clapboard library. At the end of Route 156, a beaver pond provided me a chance to discourse on my knowledge of local nature, playing the guide. The Dutch had been the first Europeans to harvest beaver here, before the New Haven Colony was even settled. Now the giant rodents are few and far between, and I had only heard the slap of their tails once, at a pond in Burlington, near the route of my first cross-state attempt.

I knew Ryan and I were walking through the Eastern Uplands area of Connecticut, from the Coastal Slope across the Mohegan Range to the Windham Hills, into the Willimantic Basin and further to the Tolland

Range. Metamorphic rock underlay most of these hills, hardier than the brownstone of the central valley, leading to the seemingly crazy jumble of small peaks and gorges that distinguished Eastern Connecticut today. I had also discovered that our route took us past the town of Moodus, which had been famous for centuries as the home of the so-called "Moodus Noises." These deep rumblings centered on Mount Tom had been interpreted as evil spirits, battles between good and evil witches, and the grinding of pearls. However, science had a more plausible explanation, that the town lay on fracture lines within the earth's crust. The subterranean rumblings were the sliding of chunks of rock far below. But as we walked along, I could feel all that information leaking out of me. There are times when natural history, geology, and archaeology break down and sunlit meadows stream unencumbered through the eyes and into the spirit.

We reached the Devil's Hopyard campground late in the afternoon, guided by chanting wood warblers. Years before, I had walked the Devil's Hopyard by myself, through tunnels of blowing white witch hazel. As I sat on the rock in the middle of Eight-Mile River, a blue dragonfly landed on my leg and sat there for a full ten minutes. A solitary glacial erratic created an open space where light rushed in and bathed me in a magical glow. My soul had felt open and clean. But I hadn't finished that long-ago walk, due to an injured back. And now while setting up camp, Ryan and I counted injuries: one small blister for me, but a few blossoming whoppers for my friend. My problems were my thighs, which had already started to go numb. Often, our physicality intrudes on glorious experience, and sometimes ruins it, as on my first trip across the state. I had to make sure that didn't happen this time.

The state park campground was primitive, but had wood and water. We ate chili and drank tea, chatted with a weekend tenter, and listened to the wonderful waterfall with its devil's hopping holes. Our only entertainment was the book *Iron John* by Robert Bly, which we read from and discussed our past failures and successes, our present virtues and troubles, and our future plans. The fire slowly grew into something magnificent. Our spirits began to wake, even as our bodies broke down.

We felt refreshed in the morning and walked around five miles on charming back roads, following blooming fernbanks, hedges, and thickets. Geese led groups of goslings across the misty morning fields. Old stills rusted in front yards and weird concrete sculptures shone in the heat. We passed through a small summer community along Lake Hayward. What time was it? How fast were we going? We didn't know and that felt very good, discussing instead morality and ethical relativism. The gray sky threatened to drench us at any moment, but never did.

These roads we walked on were well-kept macadam and meant for road traffic, not our tender feet. It was not always so here in Connecticut, which for the first hundred years of European colonization was known for its awful roads, making our state a "terrible backwater." This was changed by Yankee entrepreneurs, who created numerous private toll-roads and turnpikes. Then, in 1858 New Haven's Eli Whitney Blake invented a stone crusher that made large-scale construction of highways feasible, both here and throughout the U.S. And now many thousands of miles of paved roads blanket Connecticut, though as I have found on my walks, we have a surprising number of wonderful old dirt roads scattered all over.

On a long, straight stretch of country lane we hit the proverbial wall, due primarily to the mounting heat. Stumbling into the town of Colchester on Route 16, I quaffed a quart of Gatorade and inhaled three doughnuts, followed by a full lunch. I pleaded starvation when Ryan raised his eyebrows at this indulgence. After a quick nap on park benches in the quiet center green, we kept tramping, after being asked by a passing woman if we were "backpacking." As we contrived to answer that seemingly obvious question, she got a cell-phone call and drove off. Another questioner just shook his head when we told him our destination was Lake Williams. What would he have thought if we had told him we were headed for Massachusetts?

The Native Americans did not take such an attitude about walking. Men, women, and children would often walk hundreds of miles without too much reflection. Male adolescents would certainly have to take walkabouts before they were considered men. East of here, their new casinos at Mohegan Sun and Foxwoods belied a culture rich in physical fortitude. Above the falls of the Yantic in Norwich, not far by Indian reckoning from where I was walking that day, Chief Uncas lies buried, and with him the last of a brave attitude toward the proper use of human feet. I hoped to resurrect it, if only in my friend from Pennsylvania.

Motorcycles passed us both ways on lovely Colchester Avenue as we left town and entered the rolling countryside again. Dogs barked, chipmunks dashed, and strange white and grey ducks quacked. We did well until the last mile or two, when our feet began to burn horribly. At the broad Lake Williams, we spotted a decaying house on a small island, which Ryan promptly invented a story about. Turning onto Leonard's Bridge Road, we were confronted by a wooden bear with a fishing pole, smiling benignly at all travelers. Sheep moaned at us from roadside meadows and one eager fellow shambled over to see if Ryan had any tasty vittles.

At last we reached the blue lodge of Water's Edge family campground. The site I had reserved was gorgeous, but too far from the office. A few hundred yards felt like miles. We ate blood oranges and sandwiches for high tea and then set up the tent. Our physical needs had intruded on this day, and we groaned at the realization that we had to carry two loads of firewood from the lodge. Nevertheless, we gingerly made our way back and picked up the bundles of dry logs. As we hauled them back to our site, stopping every few yards to rest, the full impact of exhaustion hit me. Why were we bothering? We could live without a fire tonight. Was this grueling labor at the end of a demanding day really necessary?

After a break at the portable restroom, I exited and looked around. Ryan sat on a boulder on the edge of the small lake at the center of the campground, communing with the red-headed, black-feathered ducks splashing nearby. Two scuba-divers bizarrely emerged like sea-monsters from the dark water. Mysterious, mythic clouds rolled over the valley. I picked up the heavy bundle with new energy, fully aware of the importance of radiant flames for our evening activities. We needed this wood and so we struggled with it, much as we struggled with this difficult journey, to build the rich, blue bonfires in our hearts.

Chapter Thirteen
The Drop Through the Dirt

The third day of our hike developed quietly. I stretched out of the tent, reaching for the tall thick trees that surrounded the pine-needle campsite. Morning chores went smoothly, until we cooked an unappetizing breakfast of cheesy vegetable soup. I realized that last night we had made a minor error that would come back to haunt us later. A delightful fire had sprung up in the reflector pit and we had read out loud, recovering from day two's trials. But all the while, the Primus fuel bubbled away, heating the pasta and meat sauce far too long. This was the beginning of a series of problems that would take Ryan and I through *katabasis*, a Greek term we had learned from our reading of Robert Bly. It means "a descending" or "the drop through the floor."

This walk started off agreeably enough, despite this nagging doubt. Back on Leonard's Bridge Road, morning workers exited their villas, glancing curiously at us. We turned right on the reddish-brown Tobacco Road, past misty farms and half-hidden hermitages. Ryan's feet quickly began hampering him, thick with blisters, like mine on my first attempt. I had toughened my own feet purposely, and they were fine. My quadriceps, however, began to go numb immediately. At the end of Tobacco Road, we turned left and then right onto the Airline State Park Trail, which we were to follow the bulk of the day. The trail was an old railroad bed that sometimes rose up on a causeway above the surrounding forest, and sometimes dropped below like a trough.

A jogger with a dog waved at us going west, then caught us returning east, while her dog barked nervously at these strange three-legged creatures. "He can't figure out your walking sticks," she laughed. She also warned us about a detour around a farm up ahead, which was not marked on my map. Surely enough, a few miles later, a fence blocked our way and we orienteered around the tract on the rural roads. The roads were charming and broad, with soft edges for walking, but this detour added a half-mile. Near the ancient Scovell Cemetery, founded in 1733, a resident stopped his car and pointed the way. "We're having trouble with the faaaammer," he told us. Gray clouds rolled and muttered overhead as we dove back into the infinite green tunnel along the dusty, beaten track.

My pack was somehow unbalanced, and despite a few adjustments and repackings, it remained so over this entire day, adding to my discomfort. The gravel alternated from good to bad, with crunching small rocks and sharp larger rocks. I talked to Ryan about the heartening transformation of these greenways, corridors for daywalkers, bikers, and rollerbladers that keep extending and growing. But our hearts didn't seem to be in it and we walked in silence, conserving energy. Chipmunks and toads scuttled from our tromping feet. At some point we passed Ryan's record for total hiking distance, achieved with me in the White Mountains a few years earlier.

Before that, at the beginning of my Connecticut adventures, Ryan and his wife Jenifer had accompanied me on a spring hike over the entire Sleeping Giant's body, their longest walk at that time. Parking one car beyond the crumbling feet and the other beneath the proud head, we passed the area once called "The Steps" by early pioneers, looking down on Whitney Avenue, in centuries past the Farmington Turnpike, complete with guarded toll-gates.

We explored the colonnades of an old building, once the center of a huge quarrying operation. Later, when investigating this ruin's origins, I found that large portion of the brownstone in the cities of the United States once came from Connecticut. This easily quarried stone underlay the central Connecticut river valleys, while the traprock rose above it.

Some of the traprock was still quarried today, used for crushed stone in construction, but not there on the shoulder of the Giant. The words "trap rock" come from the Swedish *trappa*, which means stair, and it was easy to see how ridges like the Giant gained that nomination.

The three of us took the blue trail over the mighty head, up the tower trail, through the central plateau, into stone choked gullies, over boulder-strewn passes through the cliffs, and down an abandoned logging road, once used by teams of yoked oxen. The day was about seven miles, and we had passed that already this morning, with far heavier packs and twenty-five miles behind that.

The town of Willimantic appeared at approximately eight miles, and we found ourselves on hard sidewalks, which we avoided by treading on the new grass. This river town is known as the "Thread City" for its spool manufacturing, still evidenced by the giant spool sculptures on the main bridge. In the past, French-Canadians formed a large percentage of the town's populace, but I unfortunately heard no other languages that day. A nice lady stopped and chatted with us, while her dishrag husband and kids stared wide-eyed from their small car. Ryan felt good about this encounter, exchanging information politely, until the woman handed him a religious pamphlet. This soured an otherwise kind gesture into mere evangelism.

In the center of town, we foolishly searched for a place to sit down to eat lunch. Unfortunately, it was Sunday afternoon and nothing was open. We were several hundred yards past the only open place, Connecticut's own worldwide franchise, Subway, when we realized that we had reached the edge of town by the place the Airline Trail re-emerged. So, we flipped a coin, and Ryan lost, abandoning his pack and tramping back. Waiting for my friend to return with the sandwiches, I sprawled on the concrete in the shade of a building. People passing in cars stared at me with curiosity, and one woman asked, "Are you all right?" I had stopped caring about my personal appearance, I suppose, because none of this fazed me. When Ryan finally returned, we ate the cold and damp sandwiches on a park bench by some homeless men.

All this had wasted at least a precious hour more than we planned. It was now two p.m. and we still had fourteen miles to go, though at the time I believed it was only ten. We had run out of water and had to buy outrageously expensive bottles from the nearby movie theater, filling four thirty-two ounce bottles a bit more than halfway. That frugality turned out to be another horrible mistake.

A small boy on a wheelchair met us on the greenway just north of Willimantic. "Where are you going?" he asked.

"Up that way, to a campground." I wearily waved toward the north.

"You'll get tired!" the little boy exclaimed.

"We're already tired!" Ryan laughed.

"You could die!" the morbid kid insisted.

We laughed and continued, but he was probably right. In fact, as the sun blasted down on us with mid-afternoon fury, we began to believe it. The rail trail had been paved within the environs of town, but we carefully walked on the gravel edge instead. I had not appreciated the huge difference before. Zoned by the heat, we passed through a warehouse and strip mall district, past piles of tires and logs, and across Route 6 into the woods again. While Ryan answered the call of nature, I waited on the raised causeway. Two bicyclists rattled by on the gravel, the last people to appear for at least twelve miles. The sun went behind the trees and we set a decent pace for a while, pounding along in silence.

Clouds rumbled overhead and we quickened our stride, but could not keep it for long. We stopped every mile or so for a snack or sip of sweet water, but distance was impossible to judge on the long straightaways and gentle curves of the railroad. Rain sprinkled from the gray sky, cooling us somewhat. Stone walls flanked us now, paralleling the endless causeway. But we couldn't enjoy them. There was only one thought now, to finish. We began to see the one flaw with the wonderful greenway plan, the same problem with most of our so-called long-distance trails, lodging. Motels, campsites, bed and breakfasts? No, nothing. Why then have seventy or eighty mile trails or greenways? Why not just build ten or fifteen mile sections?

If we kept going on this path instead of turning towards a campground, we would have reached Edwin Way Teale's homestead, Trailwood, subject of his book *A Naturalist Buys an Old Farm*. The famous environmentalist and Pulitzer-Prize winner had moved there in 1959 and lived there until he died in 1980. It was now maintained by the Connecticut Audubon Society as a wildlife sanctuary and natural history museum, with over 156 acres full of trails through a variety of habitats. Teale also traveled on epic journeys, chronicling thousands of miles of observations. He once said, "Reduce the complexity of life by eliminating the needless wants of life, and the labors of life reduce themselves."[1] And Ryan and I were experiencing that reduction, speeded up, right now.

When at last we crossed a road with a visible sign, Brook Street, I stared at the map, calculating how far we had to go. Lying to Ryan and myself, I told him, "Almost there…" As we ate nuts and jerky, the skies opened and we hurriedly put on raingear. Ryan sat in a blue poncho heap on a log by the road and I desperately attempted to figure out a shorter route and distance, rain dripping on the maps. The next section sported a sign warning off travelers, but we disregarded it, plugging along on hollow legs. At this point we had about two miles left on the muddy greenway, but I told Ryan we had one.

Despite my hopeful lies, things began to go bad at this point. My legs were numb and empty and Ryan winced with each step. Near Pine Acres Lake, the trail widened, but the rain increased. At last, a barrier appeared at the top of a rare hill. We leaned against it and ate our last snack with nearly the last swallow of water. The last bit was consumed about a half-mile up the gorgeous Eleventh Section Road, which on any other day would have excited our minds and hearts. But we had no minds left. We had become machines with one purpose.

If my brain had been functioning, perhaps I would have stopped at the first stream and set up an illegal camp. But we continued, perhaps hoping that the family campground would have some sort of shelter from the downpour. Here we took the Natchaug Trail, which we planned to take north nearly to the border. The cool pine woods and meadowy horse trails looked lovely in the dim evening light, despite the rain. But we had run out of water and our mouths began to desiccate. "Mine tastes like salt," Ryan moaned. I have been in an actual desert with little water, but this was horribly different somehow. We passed a few streams, but weren't sure if they were safe. I had iodine tablets, but that would take time, time we didn't feel we had. Perhaps we already weren't thinking clearly or we might have stopped. But we had already taken many breaks and our legs were on autopilot, churning us slowly over hillocks and through heavy brush. "Never again!" Ryan snarled at me.

Reaching the road at last, I made another error, taking us left down the long forested hill to Route 198 past tiny houses with burgeoning lights. But I had turned too soon. We reached the bottom by the

Natchaug River, not at the campground, but a mile south. At last I screamed in utter exhaustion and frustration, something that made the irritable Ryan feel better. But not for long. On Route 198 the rain began to really come down, sounding like waterfalls on our already soaked heads. I tried to drink some, but my tongue was swollen and unresponsive. I began to hallucinate. "There's the sign!" I exclaimed with glee. It turned out to be a pair of mailboxes. A motorcyclist whipped by in the downpour. "Yahooo!" he shouted.

"At least someone is enjoying himself," Ryan muttered.

At nearly twenty-five miles the large, brown campground sign actually wavered into sight. We turned down the hill on a rocky dirt path, splashing through muddy rills. Inside, the office building looked like a cross between a cafeteria and a hunting lodge. But to us it was a haven of pure good. A group of children stared at us like we were freaks, which in a sense, we were.

"Is there any water?" I asked a man who seemed to be in charge.

"Sure...you can have water and coffee, over there." The man at the table, who did indeed turn out to be the owner, pointed.

Though we asked specifically for nothing else, our very beings must have cried for assistance. The group who had gotten take-out Mexican food gave us an extra dinner and a huge plate of chips. I heard one whispering that they had passed us on the road. Perhaps they felt guilty, or perhaps they were simply helping the needy. We sucked down everything regardless. I bought lemonade, then drank three coffees and two waters, taking everything the campers had to spare. A man in *katabasis* no longer feels special, privileged and we certainly did not, having become little more than helpless beggars.

We slowly set up the tent, dried off as much as possible, and unpacked sleeping bags. The kind owners let us leave our packs in the corner of the lodge to dry. Finally, we stumbled into the tent and crawled into our bags. As soon as he got warm, Ryan gleefully murmured, "I'd do that again!"

I had never seen anyone get high off of food before. "Are you crazy? I'm never doing that again!"

"I only meant..."

But I knew what he meant. This had been the most difficult day either of us had ever been through, but already the horror and humiliation were being transformed into past experience. We had survived, been taken to our lowest point, shown our utter limits. Our hearts were sobered and intensified by our descent. Being humbled once in a while is a healthy thing.

Chapter Fourteen

The Last Mile

"Share the load," I groaned, waking up and immediately quoting our favorite film. We had turned this statement into a kind of mantra, repeating it often on this seemingly endless walk. Ryan attempted to laugh, clearly still recovering from our difficult day of katabasis. We collected our bags from inside the lodge and slowly re-organized, hanging ponchos on the high boxwood hedges. I was wary of using the stove for breakfast, knowing that the last splash of fuel had to last for another two days. So, our breakfast consisted of energy bars, dried fruit, and hope.

Slowly, painfully, we hoofed up Route 198 to Peppertree Campground. Although we were continuing a few miles up the road, we stopped to check Peppertree's store anyway, having learned our lesson in Willimantic. I hailed a passing camper, "Excuse me, is the office open?" "Well, the owner's around somewhere..." Then, I used my considerable charm to beg without begging once more. I didn't really have to. The camper, Stacey, immediately offered us some of their luncheon barbecue.

"Come on," I encouraged Ryan, who had been sitting dejectedly on a stump. "These nice people are going to give us food."

"How do you do that?" he muttered rhetorically.

The family consisted of Stacey, Aaron, their dog Bud, who never stopped barking at me, and their daughter Kendra, who was polite and sweet to two filthy tramps. "I caught a big fish!" Kendra displayed her trophy to us. "Let's cook that, dad!" The small girl grinned. Stacey doled out hot dogs, hamburgers, juice, and coke, which we promptly inhaled. As if that kindness wasn't enough, she gave us a bag of food for the road, including 7 fresh oranges. We couldn't thank our rescuers enough. They had saved us the necessity of using our depleted stove and granted us a savory meal that we could never have cooked ourselves.

Ryan nearly busted a second happy button when we reached Charlie Brown Campground in no time at all. Originally, I had planned on hiking up the Natchaug Trail to a primitive campsite, but this was out of the question. I had kept this shorter option, just in case, and now was exceptionally glad, because we had the afternoon to recuperate and reorder. After checking in, we spread our wet clothes on the dry, windblown grass. Ryan made a list of our food: graham crackers, wheat and cheddar crackers, chocolate crispy sticks, moonpies, snickers, a few handfuls of Mocha Madness mix, three hempseed bars, a lonely Clif bar, dried applesauce, dried blueberries, soup, pasta, chocolate pudding, and four juice boxes. By this time we also had five oranges, but I ate one while he was making his list.

During our camp preparation, a Vietnam veteran named Robert who lived and worked at the campground introduced himself. He showed us a set of fire-starters, which the creator had imbued with napalm. "This guy's got a start on it."

I mentioned that my "fire paste" also worked well. "Goes right up!"

"But napalm! That's nasty stuff, nasty. Burn you right down to the bone."

We discussed the six pound trout he claimed to have caught earlier that day and then the thunderstorm the night before. "It sucked. It sucked," he repeated.

"It was unpleasant, that's for sure." Ryan nodded.

"Mostly unpleasant," Robert agreed.

Ryan took charge of dinner and built the fire, sharing completely in the experience at last, fully confident and experienced. Gnats and mosquitoes fled from billows of wood-smoke. But then, a rainstorm blustered in, complete with thunder and lightning. After a few attempts to keep the fire going, we retreated into the tent, where we read aloud and then settled in for an early night. Nothing exciting had happened, no great adventures had arisen, but day four had been one of conversation and

healing. My friend and I had been through something physically trau-
matic, the end was in sight, and we had connected more closely than ever.

I woke while the pre-dawn light glimmered faintly in the eastern sky.
Ryan was snoring so loud that I finally took my sleeping bag and ground
pad into a nearby pavilion, where the birds, though loud, lulled me to a
troubled half-sleep. At some late hour, Ryan peered out of the tent and
I dragged myself over, popping Pepto-Bismol and Advil, preparing for a
grim day. Then, we lathered on suntan lotion and insect repellant, our
bodies greasy and primitive. Finally, after coffee talk with Steve, the owner, we stumbled into action.

We walked a mile for a real breakfast, at the clapboard Corner Store
at the junction of Route 198 and 44. While consuming sandwiches and
Gatorade, Ryan and I had a fake discussion about whether we planned
on taking the trail option. We originally planned heading for a primitive
campground, but all our equipment was damp and lighting a fire with
wet forest wood would be, as Robert the Veteran would say, "mostly unpleasant." At any rate, I had already decided to come back and hike the
Natchaug and Nipmuck trails when I had leisure time and no finish line
to consider.

The Nipmuck trail had been named for the Indian tribe who had in-
habited the area before European incursion. It was now part of the huge
area of south-central Massachusetts and eastern Connecticut known
as "The Last Green Valley." The Quinebaug and Shetucket river valleys
formed the heart of this seven-hundred thousand acre region, crisscrossed by the ubiquitous stone walls and trails. This was a combined effort of the local people, businesses, and the National Park Service to preserve the rural character of this region, which was somehow untouched
by the gigantic Boston to Washington D.C. megalopolis. Of course, I
had found a surprising superfluity of untouched land in Connecticut as
a whole, but it was refreshing that someone was doing something to preserve part of it with this "National Heritage Corridor."

The roads in this area seemed just as worthy as the trails of our
exploration. So, after reassuring the injured Ryan, we clomped up the
macadam, taking 198 through Phoenixville. This was not the hike I had
envisioned, full of woodland odors and sudden changes of landscape.
So many of my experiences in Connecticut had been filled with magical significance that I had counted on these last two days to provide a

fascinating array of wonder. But instead we had the endless drudgery of macadam.

The only wildlife we encountered was a giant millipede in Eastford, but we did find a few farm animals. In fact, we met a horse and goat who were clearly friends, keeping company in the enclosure. "Friendships between species are absolutely miraculous," I marveled. A lonely white llama stared at us from a barn, perhaps looking for a friend of his own. Smashed frogs and snakes littered the shoulder of the road. I've never seen reptile roadkill like this, but then again I had never looked so close. At last we saw a live one, a red eft, like the one Chris and I had seen a year before on the other side of the state.

Rain threatened, but never manifested and we continued on the hot and dusty track. Near Kenyonville, we ate lunch in the gully on the side of the road, feeling like it was a friend of a kind. The road itself became more remote and forested towards the border. We stopped in a thick pine forest, which overlooked a gorgeous trout stream. This was the only real view all day, other than the rut in front of my feet. We stuck to this graveled furrow, stepping around humble roadside plants, and remarked on its changing qualities, now experts. Few will likely ever understand this strange focus on the soil at the side of the road. But we had been living there so long, we had developed our own language with it. Perhaps one day I would meet another who had tramped the highways and could speak our strange tongue, or perhaps I could teach it to others. But for now, only Ryan and I could discuss the special magic of the space between the macadam and the forest. "Share the load!" we shouted, somehow pleased that everything that usually makes a hike worthwhile had been stripped away: the views, the wild life, the mystery. We were left with merely strolling together, walking sticks firmly in our hands, towards the definite border.

Suddenly, Beaver Pines Family Campground appeared, sooner than expected. The owner let us dry our sleeping bags in the laundry room and gave us a site about 100 feet from the entrance. After hearing the tale of our marathon journey, she sweetly offered us a pop-up camper. But a mother mouse and multiple babies prevented this luxury. We attempted to catch her, the three of us scrambling foolishly throughout the trailer, but she escaped with her young through the wall.

"It feels like I'm still walking," moaned Ryan in mock horror. Now that the end was near, we had great fun comparing injuries: for me a spinal erector issue, numb left quad, swollen right knee, blisters on both index fingers, both "pointer" toes, and both little toes. Ryan's were worse: a horrifying blister wrapped around his Achilles tendon and right heel, multiple blisters underneath a callus, and several other blisters. Painful stuff, but nothing that wouldn't mend.

We lit our last and greatest fire, letting the tent dry in the wind and heat. I called the intrepid Chris and told him where to pick us up the next morning. We were forced to stop chipmunk holes with rocks and the annoyed owner chattered wildly around the campsite. We felt sympathetic and promised to remove the rocks later. But he'd have to find a new home, since this one was in the middle of the newly-opened site. For hours, the fire roared and gleamed, driving away the nefarious mosquitoes. We read out loud, ate curried lentil bisque and chocolate pudding, and discussed philosophy as the sky darkened. That night I slept well for the first time, either out of exhaustion or simply the knowledge that my long-expected journey was over.

Chris arrived at 9:00 a.m., by which time Ryan and I had woke, packed our equipment, and used the absolute last of the fuel for a breakfast of tea and applesauce. He swung his car back and forth on the gravel excitedly, saluting our effort. I stowed our packs in his trunk as he clapped Ryan on the back. Then, he drove to the border, while Ryan and I walked the last mile without the crushing weight of equipment. "Nice gully. Sandy and soft, but not too soft." We nodded. We crossed the state line by a 1906 stone marker in fine style. He went back to Pennsylvania and told his friends at work what he had done. One asked him, "why?" And he said, "if you don't know, I can't explain it to you."

I had shown Ryan the state I made my home. We had become closer than ever before and shared something unique that would bond us for life. And sharing this ending with Chris, who I had shared so many Connecticut experiences with, felt perfect. He snapped a few photos and then we piled into his car to race for home, recounting tales of our trials. I can only hope that all my last miles are shared with friends like these, and good cheer and long sleep wait at the end of the journey.

Before beginning my second hike across Connecticut, I had taken a branch and shaved the bark off, crafting a fine walking stick for Ryan. It had served him well, as had mine. Nevertheless, I had planned on snapping and burning my ancient branch at the end, feeling that it had served me long enough. Actually presented with the choice, I changed my mind. I would give the staff to someone else, pass on the wisdom of its experiences, and hopefully aid the birth of another walker. Because the people we meet, the companions we hike with, and the fellowships we create are the best gifts that nature can provide. It took me a long time to learn this simple and valuable lesson, but after this victory, it was abundantly clear. What must we do? Share the load.

Chapter Fifteen

A Night on the Mountain

I have no doubt that we were the most isolated people in Connecticut that bitter March night. Chris, Andrew, and I had driven up Route 44 through the northwest, past Haystack Mountain, which I had ascended long ago with that forgotten girlfriend who brought me to Connecticut. We reached the northwest corner of civilization in Salisbury, where we turned onto Route 41. We had a late start and it was dark already, as we crossed the border into Massachusetts and took a left on Guilder Hollow Road. Two more lefts on Jug End Road and Mount Washington Road headed us back toward the Connecticut border. The road was horribly broken by the winter frosts, with mixtures of gravel, dirt, and macadam making driving a real challenge for the fearless Chris. He and I were joined on this expedition by another SCSU teacher, Andrew. He was bright and cheerful, with a beard and glasses, looking every inch a professor, and I welcomed him gladly to our fellowship.

After numerous false signs, which I studied in dismay after leaping out of the car, we reached a huge snowbank that prevented further passage. This had to be it, or we had been led on a wild goose chase. After a moment's panic, we saw that a sign saying "Appalachian Mountain Club" hung on a nearby tree, nearly invisible in the gloom. Harpo led us into the

pitch black night, as we slopped through wet snow, the trail faintly leading along the course of a spring thaw. Our flashlights spun through the
trees, making pitifully weak arcs, sweeping over boulders and woodpiles.
"A woodpile!" I exclaimed, knowing we were close to the cabin, or at least
sort of human habitation.

The Northwest Camp, owned by the Appalachian Mountain Club,
was ours for the weekend. However, finding it in the black March night
was a challenge. At last a flashlight scanned over log walls, and we crossed
a stream, slipped up icy rocks, and found the front door. I turned on the
battered radio, and could only tune into a strange French-language station, completing a sense of dislocation and eeriness that had been gnaw-
ing at me since we had bumped onto the Taconic Plateau. Chris had no
such qualms, I'm sure. He confidently strode into the dark night with
Andrew, while I stayed with Harpo and tried to build a fire in the wood
stove. When he returned, Chris gave me stove tips and I absorbed them,
knowing his experience was gold. I boiled tea on the stove, but we used
my campstove for dinner, testing it for next summer's use. Andrew prepared the table and Chris chopped wood, making sure we had enough for
the long night. His quiet presence had become more and more a constant
in my life, and my hikes were no longer introverted affairs.

The last hike I took as a solitary walker was on Totoket Mountain
between North Branford and Durham. Totoket had a steep cliff-slope
on its north side, and a long gentle slope leading to it from the south,
so that it gave the appearance of a gigantic, cone-shaped box lid, lifting
a few hundred feet out of the earth's surface. It had once been the site of
quarries, but now was an in-between wilderness, used by locals and the
occasional walker on the Mattabessett trail.

Once I ascended to the level of the cliffs, the walk turned onto an
easy tableland, with only minor fluctuations for streambeds. A cold rain-
mist enveloped the highlands, giving the open meadows and scattered
trees a sublime spookiness. Stone farmwalls cut across the path and I
turned along one, following it to the cliff, where others joined it. At this
spot, hidden both from the trail above and from the farmlands below,
I made a small camp. Leaves swirled down from the autumn trees as I
cleared a large space for a fire. Once lit, billows of steam and woodsmoke
fought away the rain, leaving me dry and warm. Memories swirled in the
smoke as I sipped hot tea and meditated on the long path of my life.

The day burned into evening and I smothered the fire, leaving no trace that I had ever been at this quiet corner of Connecticut, though perhaps no one would approach that lonely pasture for many years. I gathered my pack and walked away from the meadows of Totoket Mountain, with a faint smile and a fond look back at the old life that had given me so much, but now must pass away.

I began to take walks more often with Chris, calling him before I planned a trek, hoping that he could join me. We hiked through the forests with the excited Harpo, who sniffed out every pile of deer scat and every squirrel hole. Sure, we saw no deer with a dog along, but she gave us a different kind of pleasure. One fine day, Chris, Harpo, and I hiked up Castle Crag in Meriden. Fire-burned meadows punctuated cedar groves and laurel tangles. Hikers passed us on their way down and sat on the cliffs above the reservoir, staring at the reflected hills in the cobalt water. Reaching the tower, Chris and I took turns ascending it for a sweeping view of south-central Connecticut, while the other held Harpo's leash as she sniffed the throngs of car-transported tourists excitedly.

We escaped the crowds at the tower and wandered out onto the big empty stretch of West Peak, the highest point of the ridge. Later, I found out that West Peak was supposedly haunted by a mysterious black dog which heralded death. Many strange and unexplained deaths had been attributed to the victims having seen this dog three times. The dog was apparently seen often, but left no tracks in snow or dirt, and barked silently at travelers of yore. Harpo was not quite as silent, as she yelped her enjoyment of our adventure. We returned to the bottom of the mountain just as the last trumpets of sunlight echoed off the cliffs.

I had also opened my heart to new opportunities. When I met a fellow English teacher at the University of Bridgeport, I made an attempt to know her, instead of withdrawing. Amy was a native of Sandy Hook, Connecticut, and had come back after graduate school in Arkansas. We traded poetry for critique, and I quickly found that hers far surpassed my own poor rhymes. But she didn't seem to think so, and we began to drive to Fairfield for lunch and discussion. We found many things in common besides poetry: music and film, coffee and tea, travel and photography. Then I escorted her to the Niantic Book Barn for our first official date, and a tree took root.

We began walking almost immediately, but I was careful to balance my love of this activity with other, more traditional pursuits. So, I took her to Sherwood Island, Connecticut's first state park, for a sunset picnic. We found a hidden spot on the edge of the peninsula and ate sun-dried tomatoes, blood oranges, and cheese on crackers with hot pepper spread. A group of local children rambled by and I chatted with them amiably. Amy laughed at my valiant attempt to use glassware on the windy beach, and we used our tea-mugs for a splash of red wine.

As the sun disappeared behind the hills, Amy began snapping pictures of Long Island Sound. As we walked back toward the parking lot, we found a marvelous beech tree, which Amy circled and photographed comprehensively. "I love this tree!" she exclaimed. The dropping sunlight turned the tree green, then yellow, then orange. She lay on the cool evening grass and speared her lens toward the color-shifting beech, smiling broadly at me, her eyes changing from blue to green to gray, and I felt myself falling toward her, helpless before the power of genuine human connection.

In the cabin on Bear Mountain a month later, Chris, Andrew, and I sipped whiskey and talked of other times. I told my friends the story of the day I hiked along the tilted, rusty-orange cliffs of Mount Higby and watched a massive lightning-storm crawl across the highways. Running two miles to my car, I passed two elderly British ladies struggling up the slope. "Better go back, there's a storm coming!" I told them. "We'll be all right, luv," they assured me. After unsuccessfully pleading with them, I reached my waiting car just as the sky opened in a torrent of freezing water and crackling electricity. "The question of those women's fates haunts me still," I told my friends, enjoying the role of storyteller, feeling that my Connecticut experiences were being shared with others who understood.

I woke up long past midnight with a need to expel the whiskey. Sighing, I stumbled out into the inky forest, my flashlight searching for the toilet. As the beam swung into the distance, it lit two red eyes briefly. I swung it back and the red eyeshine stared at me, too low to be a deer, too high to be a raccoon. A coyote? A bear? The spirit of death? Whatever it was, I believed it signaled ill for me, and as I hurriedly returned to the relative safety of the log cabin, I knew the cause. Chris would be leaving Connecticut in a few short months and I wasn't ready. I had only begun to fully appreciate the rare worth of our friendship and emerge from the shell of my solitude to enjoy dinners with his wife Alison and walks with

Harpo in the evening. It often happens thus, that only when something is lost do we realize what we had. I thought of Amy and knew I wouldn't let it happen again. So, I said farewell to Chris in May, and raced up the next summer's trail, following the faint tracks of the future.

Chapter Sixteen

Companionship

With Amy as my new companion, I explored Connecticut like it was another country, seeing trees and birds for the first time. We camped in Connecticut for the first time at Macedonia Brook. The day before we stopped at the nearby White Silo Winery, sampling their excellent blackberry and rhubarb wines in the cool cellar of an old barn surrounded by local art. What I hadn't known when I had visited White Silo with Chris, so many years ago, was that this was only one stop on the extensive Connecticut Wine Trail. The tasting of fine local wines would become one of our shared passions, one that was not separate from love of the land itself. Amy introduced me to this other, more epicurean trail and allowed me to see Connecticut though yet another lens.

After buying a few bottles, we had come to this hidden haven in the western woods. She had never ventured into this peaceful hanging valley, though she had grown up in Sandy Hook, only twenty miles away. She often told me, "I can't believe I didn't know all this existed." I was happy to play my part.

Finding a secluded site at the end of a gravel road, we set up my tent and ate a snack before taking a walk on the shady, stone-walled track that once heard the clop of horse-hooves. I had walked on this path by myself, during those long, lone years, and I marveled at how far I had come, and how changed my life was now. Amy and I had revisited many of my former haunts, and each ghostly memory was now populated with a living form.

The first return was to Beacon Cap, an easy, initiation hike that I took her on when still unsure of her ability or desire to hike. The orange forest was just about to April into green, and the tree-trunks glittered with afternoon sunlight. After a ramble through the luminous woods, I led her to the mushroom-shaped glacial erratic that gave the hill its name. We boiled tea, had sandwiches and chips, and I lit a rather large fire in the lee of the boulder – the wood was very dry and birch bark sent the whole thing up easily. Then, I convinced her to follow me up the seemingly sheer side of mushroom cap rock. Once up, she lost any fear and kissed me with joy at the view and the accomplishment. We lounged there in the sun and I told her of my previous hikes, wanting her to understand the layers of personal history that had led me to her.

Another revisitation was Roaring Brook Falls on the Quinnipiac Trail. I had gone there a year before with Chris and Harpo, before my friend left for California. We had built a small fire and met another hiker and his Belgian Shepherd, which the much-smaller, but always brave Harpo promptly attacked. I told this story to Amy as we hiked over the undulating ridge, which I had been told was caused not by glaciers, but by erosion due to overgrazing, when sheep roamed bare hills. Now they were nearly all forested, though we did pass the grassy clearing of a horse farm. A coyote howled in the distance and was answered by furious dog barks from the farm, but both were lost to our hearing as we picked our way through groves of stunted cedars.

Reaching the hollow that had been created by previous incarnations of the stream, Amy gleefully photographed the pretty waterfall, not realizing that it was the small one. Depositing the pack by the huge firepit used by modern horseriders, I showed her the cascade that continued to carve a gorge in the ridge, then led her down the hill to a view of the larger falls, at seventy feet the longest single drop in the state, incongruous in the suburbs of Cheshire. I had seen these falls many times, but sitting on a log watching them splash down the cliff with the laughing Amy warmed and augmented all memory.

At Macedonia Brook she lit the fire, doing a great job with wet wood, giving us more practical light and heat. I swept the campsite and cooked a simple meal of pasta in vodka sauce. The night became cold, but we pulled camp chairs close to the fire, resting boots on the rock ring. With head-lamps aglow, we read each other poetry aloud, while the forest fell asleep around us. Our collaboration flowed naturally and easily. "I was instantly comfortable with you," Amy told me, and I agreed. She enhanced each outdoor experience because of this connection, but even more with her preternatural ability to find the unexpected. The list of firsts increased every day: my first wild beaver, my first bear track, my first bluebird...

The bear track incident occurred on our third hike in the People's State Forest south of Riverton. We had stayed at the Old Riverton Inn the night before, after taking photos of the huge Pinchot Sycamore along the Farmington River and the twisted Granby Oak. These two trees were the champions of their kind in Connecticut and the Pinchot was in fact the largest single tree. Amy admired the mottled bark of the sycamore and climbed onto the coiled limbs of the magnificent oak. We had also hiked briefly at the wild Ender's Falls and rescued a sapling that had been trapped by the fallen trunk of a larger tree. Amy seemed to be impressed with my strength when I heaved the huge log aside, and I was impressed with her compassion and consideration for the tree, which I would have probably left to its fate without her urging.

After breakfast in the antique carriage-stop inn, we drove to the desolate, snow-choked trailhead. The woods were thick with tracks, includ-ing many sizes of stags, does, and fawns. I pointed out zigzagging dog tracks and tried distinguishing them from what I was sure were purpose-ful, straight-lined coyote prints. We learned tree species together and I showed her how birch bark can be used to start a fire. And then, she pointed at a subtle track that I had walked past. "What's that?" I stared at it. "That's a bear track." Amy seemed pleased, but I was stunned. I had spent years searching the winter woods for bear tracks, and she had found one right away.

Perhaps she had some sort of divine providence, since these occa-sions seemed too frequent to explain logically. Like the spring day we drove to the Larsen Nature Sanctuary to revisit the wildlife that I had found and shown my students on two previous hikes. We walked slowly and quietly through the budding woods, and found the deer herd grazing by a stone wall. They stared at us with fright and slowly, then quickly, retreated through the woods, showing us twelve white tails bouncing across the forest's periphery. After several woodpecker sightings, we spotted the first bluebird either of us had seen, and Amy crept up on it with a natural patience I had taken so long to teach myself.

I thought that oft-visited Sleeping Giant was a completely known factor before I took Amy there. The first hike was on a hot July day, and although we saw a garter snake and a toad, I felt that the magic had not touched her, steamed from our skin by the unusual humidity. However, on our second jaunt around the mountain on an unusually balmy February day, she led me to Mount Carmel Spring Falls, which up until that point I had considered something of a myth. Enhanced by recent snows, it cascaded down a sheer face for fifty feet, having worn a narrow channel in the limestone. According to all reports, this was a mere trickle even at the best of times, but this was a full-blown waterfall, with white liquid rushing into the hanging valley below. Agape, I had walked around this wonder, not quite believing this luck. Amy smiled beatifically, as if she had planned the encounter, though she had never been to the Giant without me.

She was more than a good luck charm for my wanderings, though. All these returns gave new life to each Connecticut place. Amy's presence made being afoot the unequaled pleasure I always hoped for, just as it did that early autumn evening at Macedonia Brook State Park. As I drifted off into a fire-warmed sleep, I smiled happily. Everything old was new again, and adventures would follow.

We slept long, completely at home in the birdsong woods, then struggled out of our sleeping bags into the crisp mountain air. After breakfast of black tea, oatmeal, and dried blueberries, we took down the tent and I shouldered the pack. We each grabbed a walking stick and headed directly from the site through the forest to the old grassy road. From there we hiked up a steep slope, clambering over boulder jumbles, and reached the ridge overlooking eastern New York. There we sat on a ledge and ate apples and chocolate. I talked to her of my fishing experience here and she told me of her family camping trips to Hamonnasset. On Cobble Mountain we continued along a ridge trail that promptly disappeared. Nonplussed, we crept down a nearly vertical slope. Amy seemed worried, but I expounded on the wonders of getting lost, giving her the wise lessons I thought I learned in my years of hermitage.

And then it happened – something frightfully new and unexpected, something horrifying. "Ow!" Amy exclaimed as she followed me down a steep eroded area of dirt and roots.

"What happened?" I turned around.

"A bug flew into my eye!" And then, "Ow!" she cried again.

Moving quickly, towards her, I immediately saw the cause – a cloud of fierce bees. "You've stepped on a bees' nest! Quick, this way." I sprang into action, grabbed her walking stick, and tried to pull her down the slope as quickly as possible without breaking our ankles. Pulling my fleece from the backpack, I swiped at the sluggish but vast cloud of bees that was attempting to crawl underneath her clothes. One of the single-minded warriors stung me on the wrist, but Amy cried out with a seemingly endless succession of painful stings.

As soon as we seemed to be far enough away from the disturbed nest, I stopped her on a flat boulder and hastily crushed the remaining insects, stripping her down and finding two underneath her shirt. She was crying now, scared, and I endeavored to calm her, knowing that the poison in her veins could be deadlier in an anxious state.

"Are you allergic?"

"No," she sobbed, and relief washed over me. She wasn't going to die. Nevertheless, we were lost in the woods, far from the car, and even farther from the town of Kent.

"It hurts," Amy stated simply, and my heart nearly broke.

"We've got to get out of here. Can you walk?"

"I think so." And so, my love for her guiding me like a spear, I found a deer trail in a hanging hollow and followed it back to the grassy road, where we stepped quickly in the direction of the campsite. I interjected comforting words, cursing the bees. "It wasn't their fault," she said, and in amazement at her grace and wisdom, I demurred. How could she be so forgiving, so understanding? I could see her pain, multiplied the one throbbing sting on my wrist by twenty and shuddered.

We reached the car, I jolted onto the gravel, and zoomed to the Park Office. They had nothing for bee stings, but the very young ranger directed me to the grocery store in Kent. I broke all traffic laws and ran inside, buying everything they had that was remotely appropriate. I treated her injuries the best I could and headed home, where a paste of baking soda was concocted and applied again and again. The next few days were spent recovering from the incident, which I feared would put an end to our forays into the forests. But I underestimated Amy, and the healing power of walking in Connecticut. We returned to the places I loved and I marveled at her resilience. And this incident, though it seemed like disaster, became another story in our shared adventure.

Chapter Seventeen

The Winds of October

Afternoon waves at Hammonasset State Park grasped at the tufted dunes, driven forward by a stiff wind from the southwest. Amy and I wandered along this windswept beach, trying to catch a sunset on the Sound, rare for busy people like us. The wind teared our eyes as we tried to watch a gang of parasurfers leap off the waves into the salt air. Before our walk we had escaped the persistent wind in our tent, boiling hot chocolate and munching on berries. That repast served us well on the exposed dunes, with high tide crashing at our feet and the offshore gale whipping through our hair. She brushed back a strand of her red-brown hair and smiled.

The sparrows arrived with her the previous spring. For the ten years before Amy arrived, I lived in empty apartments and houses, devoid of most life. One lonely plant, a refugee from my brother's wedding, hunched pathetically in the corner. In the twenty years before that, I had no pets of my own, no plants in my small rooms, no bird feeder in the back yard. In my cyberpunk youth, I had no problem with this. I thought people could live in a sterile, modern, convenient world, drawing sustenance from plastic-bagged food and machine-conditioned oxygen. Later, when this seemed inadequate, I fled those bare rooms, not even realizing

I was fleeing, heading into the wooded areas of the suburbs, or farther afield to mountains and rivers, beaches and seas. But I still had no awareness that something was wrong at home, with the way I lived day to day. It never even occurred to me that the sterile, bacteria-free kitchen, or the white, museum-like bedroom was in some way destroying me.

Then Amy moved into a condominium with me, and everything changed. A feeder appeared on my porch, bringing blue jays and cardinals, starlings and titmice, a lone flicker. Sparrows nested in the eaves. Mourning doves cooed us awake. We added suet in the winter and were blessed with chickadees and juncos, hopping brightly in the snow. The meager garden sprang to attention with the bulbs she planted and nurtured through the dry months: daffodils, crocuses, peonies, hyacinths, and tulips. I grew to love the so-called weeds, so varied and versatile in their uses and appearance. Squirrels and chipmunks fed from our bounty, peeking into the windows with friendly hunger. A groundhog we named Woody lived under the neighbor's porch, and soon had a wife and child, romping in the grass and bounding through the bushes.

Inside, plants stretched their ropy limbs into every corner. Rooms became animate with blue ice plants and cacti, jade plants and bamboo, devil's ivy and peace lilies, living beside various species of spider plants. We exchanged oxygen and carbon dioxide in the definitive symbiotic relationship, so obvious and yet disregarded by my former self. A twenty-gallon fish tank graced the living room, bringing the domestic concept of "daily feeding" into my consciousness, which until now had been responsible for no life but its own. The marigold swordtails and black-finned tetras were joined by rare fish from New Guinea, all swimming in harmony under the lights, gratefully accepting my feedings, schooling together near the glass whenever I ventured nearby. We made plans for cats, for those mammalian companions I had longed for in my childhood, to complete the domestic ecosystem that now surrounded me.

In a few short months, Amy had brought life to the house in a way I never knew. And I realized my constant urge for the wilderness was satisfied right here. We need green and growing things, somewhere deep in our DNA. No walls of pressed board and lung-cutting insulation can keep them out. I was arrogant to think that I could fight my biology, but more importantly I was wrong to think that the sanitized existences so many of us have is superior in some way. Sure, our air-conditioned mod-

ern life protects us from the elements and the more aggressive bugs and
humans, but why had I kept out the rest of the natural world? The home
I now shared with Amy and her menagerie has become part of the world,
rather than an escape from it.

Amy had also brought me back to the seashore, giving it back to me
in a way that I hadn't known since my youth, since I turned away from
it a decade before. We sunbathed at Rocky Neck State Park, watched
sailboats race amongst the Thimble Islands, and dunked our heads in
the waves at Bluff Point's pebbled beach. We took walks in Stratford
to search for shells and investigated the mysterious green parrots that
had puzzled me years earlier, hanging off their non-native twig-castles.
And like those sanderlings I watched at Milford Point long ago in what
seemed another age, I learned the techniques of clamming, digging into
the soft sand and closing searching fingers on the slippery shellfish, who
retreated from me like the past itself.

At Hammonasset that October day, the great sphere of ruby finally
sank over Long Island, and we strolled back through the mainly deserted
campground. A few brave groups huddled around fires, quilted blankets
draped over their legs, sipping hot drinks. They, too, had come to this
post-season campground, drawn by the same thing we had been. What
was it? I wasn't sure, and perhaps it was foolish stubbornness to want to
draw out the summer with an autumn camping trip on Connecticut's
browning shore.

Back at the tent, I cooked soup and tea, while Amy prepared sleeping
bags and warmer clothes for the sub-zero night. The branches of wind-
wracked pines swayed around the tent as we burrowed slowly into our
bags, munching on crackers and filling hot water bottles. We read poetry
aloud to each other in the dim tent to stave off the cold and wind, to light
the growing darkness. Finally, as the wind died down, we drifted off into
a pine-scented sleep.

In the morning, frost had settled on the rain-fly and we shivered our
way to boiling water for coffee and oatmeal, shoveling needed fuel into
our inner furnaces. The sun finally warmed our faces and we headed out
to the beach again, where fishermen hopefully cast into the surf, a group
of budding scientists took notes on the local nature, and a grizzled artist
set up his easel in the morning sun. Cormorants sped across the wave-
tops, so calm now after last evening's fury. Snowy egrets speared fish in

a wading pool, wood ducks dove for minnows with wiggling tails, and a great blue heron wheeled across the brown expanse of the salt marsh slowly, searching for breakfast.

These shore birds were already hard at work, and though they seemed freer, would spend the majority of their time on survival. They would tell me that it was not foolishness that brought me to Hammonasset in October. Such days we must steal from the autumn of work, the endless paper trails and e-mails, the demands of bosses and families. We must snatch them now, before the real cold sets in, the cold that does not respond to steaming mugs of hot chocolate.

I was already preparing for winter in another way. What Amy didn't know that October day was that hidden at home in a drawer was a ruby ring that I had spent months choosing. I planned to send her postcards with clues, leading to a surprise January vacation, and a question in a park in a faraway city. I guessed she would say yes, I hoped with all my heart, and I kept my secret all that autumn.

Before the drive from magical Hammonasset back to the condominium we now shared, Amy and I stopped at Elizabeth's Café in Madison for Eggs Benedict and a goat-cheese omelet. The woman next to us discussed death with the café manager, having lost her father-in-law only two days earlier. "But he was old and lived a good life," she said promptly. *A good life,* I thought, *we always say that. What does it mean?* And as the woman I loved smiled at me across the table, her cheeks rosy with a weekend well-spent, I knew.

Chapter Eighteen
The Trail of White Blazes

I'd long considered the northwest corner of Connecticut, peppered with Bed and Breakfasts and camping opportunities, the ideal place for a long-distance hike. Now that I had hiked across the state from border-to-border, the rich Litchfield Hills seemed to me to be the place to take Amy for our own adventure. In this case, the number of routes to take seemed endless, but we finally decided on a section of the Appalachian Trail.

Amy was a little surprised that in all my treks in Connecticut, I had only taken small slices of this fabled footpath. Completed in 1937, the "AT" unit of the National Park Service crosses fourteen states, six national parks, eight national forests, and 6501 feet of elevation. It was the brainchild of Benton MacKaye, a forester who proposed it as a project of regional planning. But the volunteers who had put it together were the real heroes, and they have left something miraculous, a 2175 mile corridor that takes the hundreds of hikers who complete the full length every year approximately five million footsteps. Amy and I would walk only thirty-two miles of this world wonder, at least for now.

We began the day at our new home in Hamden, peering out into a drizzling rain that seemed to bode ill for the hike. Amy's brother, Mike, along with his wife Liz and his daughter Julia, drove along with us so that we could drop my car at Race Brook Lodge just over the border in Massachusetts. Then, they drove us back to the trailhead in West Cornwall, where our journey was set to begin. Along the way we enjoyed the turkeys and cows, farms and fields, along with Julia's new obsession with rabbits. "Bring me a rabbit!" She demanded of us, knowing her birthday was the next weekend. "How about they bring you a picture of a rabbit?" Liz groaned. We promised we would.

After our noble drivers dropped us off, we put Vaseline on our feet and saddled up the packs. Although we had no camping gear, we did have "nice" clothes and extra shoes along, for eating at the fancy taverns. Amy had eased me into an appreciation of some of the finer things Connecticut had to offer, after years of beef jerky and dried fruit. Just a week earlier we had enjoyed *A Funny Thing Happened on the Way to the Forum* at the famous Ivoryton Playhouse, followed by a lovely meal of duck and salmon at the award-winning Copper Beech Inn. We had stared out the Inn window at the fantastic beech in the yard, possibly the oldest in the nation, and talked of our love of these remarkable trees.

Now, we walked in another beech forest, slipping through narrow cracks in huge boulders, and struggling up the edge of the plateau through a misty rain. Our legs burned with the new activity, inevitable when beginning a hike with heavy loads. At the top of the hill in Pine Swamp, the beeches gave way to birch trees and blueberry bushes, and we wished time to speed ahead to their annual ripening. We trudged through the leafy tunnel, brightened to a neon lime color by the rain. Wood thrushes and nuthatches zipped through the underbrush, performing spring rites. I spotted predator scat, some coyote, some bigger and unidentifiable. Bear? Probably—we were in their country now. Amy found Jack-in-the-pulpits barely preaching, and red ladyslippers. "My mom loved them," she said sadly. "That's a good sign."

We ate lunch and continued up Mount Easter, through groves of enormous ferns, and across quartz meadows. A few of the 165,000 white blazes led us on, and we passed a thru-hiker heading south towards Harper's Ferry, West Virginia. "Stop at the Toymaker's Café in Falls Village," he told us. After this amiable encounter, we began to hear the car engines at Lime Rock Park, which was celebrating its fiftieth year of racing. It was an incongruous sound to accompany us through the wet, empty woods. We stopped for a second lunch with the cars racing below us and mountain ranges stretching away into the gray distance. We had a long way to go.

Continuing along Sharon Mountain and passing a deer skull, I told Amy childhood stories to take her mind off her now aching knees. My old left thigh injury from that long-ago first cross-Connecticut attempt also began acting up, and I hoped it wouldn't get worse. Our boots crossed slippery streams and sank into red, pine-needle hillsides. We applied insect repellant and drank cool, fresh water without thinking, completely in tune with the trail-world that I had worked to understand years before.

Soon, we traveled off the plateau, through groves of massive white pines and burst from the green tunnel onto Route 7. Hooking around a cornfield and along the Housatonic River before crossing it, we turned left past Housatonic Valley High School and along Warren Turnpike, finally pushing into the forest again. We had passed the turn-off to the Mohawk Trail, which I explained to Amy had once been part of the AT. Our legs wobbled beside the railroad tracks, but took us past the "Falls Village, 1739" sign and into one of the least densely populated towns in the state. There we found our reserved lodging, which shall remain nameless, as it was entirely empty. An envelope with our keys awaited, but the tavern was abandoned and there was nowhere else in the village center to eat dinner. This was not what we wanted to find after a calorie-burning hike.

When we limped outside after a shower, two locals asked us if the inn was actually open. We explained the situation and they informed us that the nearest place was over a mile away. "We'll give you a ride, and I'm sure someone will drive you back." We agreed and introduced ourselves to Steve and Carlo, and their Scottie-dog, Max, who ushered us into an open top Jeep with a boat attached. It was a bit on the brisk side, but we didn't complain as these two were our saviors. Gorp and dried fruit had been great for lunch, but we needed real food now.

Steve and Carlo dropped us at the Mountainside Café, where we received a table and a prompt dinner of New England clam chowder, fish and chips, and a hamburger for Amy. We scarfed it all down and bought cookie bars to go. "I have an unusual request," I told the waiter, and explained our situation once again. "I'm sure someone can take you," he assured us. Turned out the owner, Tom, could take us, and in a short while we jumped into his black pick-up. He told us that the owners of our mysteriously empty lodging had absconded to Rhode Island, and were trying to sell the place. "Nice of them to tell us," I laughed, full of food and not caring much now. We had been blessed by what Appalachian Trail hikers call "trail magic." Perhaps Amy was right about those ladyslippers being good luck.

Back at the inn, we found a lack of heat problematic, but piled blankets from the empty rooms on the bed. Our suite was actually quite beautiful, but in the freezing night it lost a little charm. In the morning, we walked in a pouring rain to the Toymaker's Café and had a fabulous breakfast of French toast, a ham and egg sandwich, and life-giving coffee. The couple next to us saw our "breakfast voucher" and asked Amy if we had been at the "freezing inn." They had come in late last night and were also confused and disappointed.

This disappointment combined with the rainstorm gave me my only doubts. I remembered those other hikes across Connecticut, the problems and struggles, and considered briefly taking the flatter, shorter roads to Salisbury. But Amy was all for continuing as planned, and as we crossed the famed "Iron Bridge," the rain stopped. Fishermen cast their lines into the deep pools of the Housatonic, and I told Amy about my own fishing experiences with my father. We stopped at the "Great Falls," a truly impressive sixty-foot drop, full of spring glory. I had somehow never seen this wonder of Connecticut, and I marveled at the continuing revelations that await anyone who just slows down and looks for them.

We followed the white marks across the road and were immediately rewarded with a sunlit meadow of touching beauty. Then, it was a steady uphill climb through fairytale forests of huge maples and pines, broken by fields of chickweed and wild columbine. A huge centipede scuttled across the rocks. We heard turkeys and red-winged blackbirds, and then a strange yelping. "Sounds like a puppy," Amy said. "Sort of," I mused, and we debated for a bit, until we realized that it was a puppy, or rather a hungry coyote pup, hidden in the brush nearby.

We continued up and up until we reached an open section that looked over an idyllic valley. We ate mangoes and nuts, resting before the next leg of the journey. A grandfather, father, and son passed by and we chatted about the day. "If it were easy, everyone would be up here," the father noted. Amy and I continued, waiting for the next uphill climb that would take us to the top of Mount Prospect. After a ridge walk through more thick pines and meadows, we reached a sign that read "Mt. Prospect, .5 miles" —but in the direction we had come. We were already over four miles into the day's hike and had passed the only difficult ascent. Surprised, we gleefully set off again, and immediately our mood intensified at Rand's View, one of the best spots on the Connecticut AT, where we could see our third day's walk on the Taconic Plateau stretching northwards.

We strode through a weird, moss-encrusted area on the way to Raccoon Hill, where we encountered the strange, cobbled limestone outcrop called the Giant's Thumb. It looked very much like a standing stone of Europe, and I could see how early legends of a Viking settlement had sprung up around it. At Billy's View, named for a local farming boy, we ate goldenberries and the huge cookie squares from the Mountainside Café and talked about the nice people we had met in Falls Village. A look at the map showed that we were crossing a cable that had been laid down during the Cold War as part of the nationwide defense system. This reminded us of a recent hike on the Metacomet Trail, where we had explored the abandoned Nike missile site and then napped on the cliffs of Rattlesnake Mountain.

A short walk later, on Wetauwanchu Mountain, scarlet tanagers flitted through the treetops and woodpeckers pattered on dead snags. I showed Amy a healthy conifer that had been clawed by a bear. All these predators, and not one deer track yet, despite the mud. They must have been hiding well, somewhere amongst the thorny thickets and old stone walls. At last we reached the final cliff switchbacks that took us down to Route 44, and Amy's knees began to ache again. But we were almost done, and breezed down the road to reach Salisbury at the ridiculously early time of 2:30. There was no question in our minds that it was time for afternoon tea, and we crossed the road to ChaiWalla, recommended to us by Steve and Carlo, finding it busy with a late Sunday lunch crowd. But after a short wait we were seated and inhaled Sherpa tea, potstickers, and a scone with lemon curd.

After this relaxing interlude, we headed back to the White Hart Inn and were greeted warmly. At our room, we showered and napped, before stumbling to the Tap Room for dinner. Glasses of cool white wine and dinners of grilled game hen and butternut squash tortellacci reinvigorated us, and we talked excitedly of the next day, and of our wedding plans for autumn. A ruby engagement ring sparkled on Amy's finger in the candlelight like a spring beech leaf, and I couldn't decide whether the ring or the distance on the map showed more truly how far we had come.

The next morning we had a quick breakfast and quickly tramped up the road past the yellow "hiker crossing" sign, knowing that there was a long trail ahead of us, which I had estimated at thirteen miles, but turned out to be more than fourteen. The first leg up to Lion's Head led through fields of asters and wild ginger, beeches and oaks. The sun warmed our bodies at we struggled up steep zigzags and finally reached the peak. "Look how sky the blue is!" Amy laughed. I showed her the place we had dropped off of Wetauwanchu, the bulge of Mount Prospect, and the long ridge of day one.

The two of us strode across the hump of the Taconic Plateau, which had been worn down from a gigantic, ancient mountain of long ago. We crossed mossy boulder-choked streams, passing painted trillium and mountain laurel thickets. Reaching Riga Junction in just a few hours, we started up Bear Mountain, which was the only section of the hike I had done before. A school group passed us on their way down and we reached the summit cairn while wind whipped our jackets. We tied a colorful prayer flag to a birch tree in the tradition of the Buddhists and rambled down the steep, rocky trail, hanging on to pitch pines and scrub oaks, telling stories as we walked, helping each other to find those moments that make life extraordinary.

Beyond that lay the old growth forest of Sage's Ravine, the grueling ascent and descent of Mount Race, and the eagle soaring below us in the updrafts. We would find a fresh bear print in the mud, a chorus of coyotes exploding on a cliff not fifty feet away, and a final rest at the rustic Race Brook Lodge. We had yet to snap the miraculous photo of a jackrabbit bounding across Route 41 as we marched the last hundred yards of our thirty-two miles, saving it for Julia's birthday party as a special treat. But all that lay in a future yet unwalked on the slopes of Bear Mountain. For now, Amy and Eric were wandering on the woody margins of Connecticut, somewhere between beginning and end, heading for the border.

Chapter Nineteen

A Home of Green Hills

The house Amy and I share now is full of images, on trails and lookouts across the state, images of strength, of summer, of hope. One in particular, a black and white photograph of the two of us on top of Beacon Cap in the Naugatuck State Forest, draws me. Every time I pass it, I think of naturalist John Burroughs's essay "The Exhilarations of the Road," in which he says, "The roads and paths you have walked along in summer and winter weather, the fields and hills which you have looked upon in lightness and gladness of heart, where fresh thought have come into your mind, or some noble prospect has opened before you, and especially the quiet ways where you have walked in sweet converse with your friend, pausing under the trees, drinking at the spring—henceforth they are not the same; a new charm is added; those thoughts spring there perennial, your friend walks there forever."[1]

Perhaps the photograph does not really tell me that much. Perhaps I am thinking back to all the days we have spent walking the Connecticut paths together. We strolled on the rail trail near Newtown, boiling tea on a snow-covered picnic table. We discovered a strange gravel road in Naugatuck that skirted a train track and led to the steep and isolated Spruce Brook Ravine. We found the small onion-domed chapel of St.

Sergius, the only remnant of the Russian Village in Southbury, founded by Leo Tolstoy's son as a haven for fleeing writers, artists, and musicians. We hiked past new housing developments on the Mattabessett Trail, watched warily by a broad-winged hawk, then ate lunch in Cognichaug Cave, while chickadees nested above in the cliff-cracks. Often, we would stop walking and simply sit and watch cardinals fighting in the willows by a pond, or ducks pairing up to begin annual mating.

With Amy by my side, I began to find new connections with the rest of the world, as well. She brought me into the cities of Connecticut, sad-ly ignored due to my earlier yearning for solitude. We strode around "hat city" Danbury for a charity walk and explored the crannied bookstores of New Haven. She held my hand as we rambled past the beeches and sycamores of Beardsley Park in Bridgeport, past the graves of huckster P.T. Barnum and the famous comedian Tom Thumb, past taverns where General Washington stayed and the city hall where Abraham Lincoln gave an address. We marveled at the Monets of the Hill-Stead Museum of Farmington and the Manets at the Wadsworth Athenaeum. We wan-dered around Greenwich before a lecture at the Bruce Museum, strolled the streets of old Norwalk after exploring the Aquarium, and ambled along poet Wallace Stevens' daily walking route in Hartford.

What's next? There are so many options. I'm looking at the far east-ern section, heading north from beautiful Stonington on the Narragan-sett and Pachaug Trails, up scenic Route 169, and on the old reliable Airline Trail to the very northeast corner of the state. But I'd like to start a new tradition. With good maps and handbooks, we could walk from lodging to lodging, without a plan or purpose. We'll use the extensive trail networks and back roads to lead us to new lands and new experi-ences.

I've already walked such a long, green trail that now I have to write things down to remember them. On a day that now seems lifetimes ago, I explored the blocked entrance of an abandoned cobalt mine at the base of Great Hill in East Hampton. A group of teens parked nearby, smok-ing and giggling, reminding me of my past schoolboy self, of the lives I lived before Connecticut. Later, eating fruit on the overlook ledge high above, I saw a glimpse of the future I was now living. A couple sat fishing on a boat in a small lake below, surrounded by ancient trees of surpassing flower. Small, white houses with docks lined the shores, and I saw myself among them, in a future that is now here, living a quiet life filled with books and walks, amidst the green woodland hills.

I resisted Connecticut at first, thinking it was just a waystation, another formless and mythless land in which I would bide my time. It seemed to have no essential identity like certain other, more famous states. But I found instead in my personal story and the stories of Ryan, Chris, Amy, and thousands of others that this seemingly minor state was a place of transformation, of beauty, of strength. Connecticut taught me to not look towards distant lands, but to live here and now, in the center of a spinning wheel of time.

These moments cannot be found with cars, or trains, or airplanes. Only by touching the earth, connecting with it, and earning these memories have they truly become part of me. As I tramp across the asphalt and dirt, under the green spring trees, or over russet autumn leaf-piles, the geography of connection comes unbidden. This is the place I grew into a person more fully myself. Where I gave up my childish search for meaning and began to follow deer through the forest. It is a land where I taught thousands of students and made dozens of friends, finding unlooked for companionship. Occasionally, we need solitary interludes, to relax or to gain strength. But sharing the journey makes everything more worthwhile. Why else take pictures or tell stories to our friends? Why else would I record these quiet adventures for you to read?

I sometimes think I should become a teacher of walkers, because there are so many images to share. So much to learn from and enjoy right here: ruins in the woodlands, the dry noon earth, stands of green pines punctuating gray woods, a lone hiker resting on a hilltop, a butterfly sipping a flower, and the richness of passing time. And so many that want to learn! Families milling about the trailheads, staring hopefully at the summer sky. Birders sitting on chairs by the ponds, waiting for that perfect sighting. Joggers and cyclists traveling swiftly on the growing greenway system. And new friends and students, unaware of the unexpected wilderness in the backyards of cities. When their unsure feet begin to fail, I must teach them to persevere, to absorb the profound wisdom of our environment, to join me in the enchanting colonial wilderness of Connecticut.

And then, as velvet shadows deepen around a camp-fire, our oldest memories and deepest instincts will hopefully revive. The wind and

birds may whisper to us the mightiest of secrets. We will take a walk by
moonlight along a dry stream-bed, over a distant hill seen all our lives.
The ancient track will intensify our memories, opening tired eyes to subtle movements and events. Only then can we become part of the great
silences of nature in which we tread.

Here in Connecticut I have done away with the busy pursuits of
youth and found the green heart of life. In this land of little hills and rivers, the constant trees welcome me time and time again. These paths all
have the same smell. My boots ring on these stones with the same note.
I have found something lost in childhood—the myth of home.

Notes

Epigraph and Chapter 19

Burroughs, John. "The Exhilarations of the Road." Winter Sunshine. *The Writings of John Burroughs.* Boston: Houghton, Mifflin & Co., 1904-22.

Chapter Two

1. Turner, Alfred Milford. Report of the State Park Commission For the Two Fiscal Years Ending in 1916 (Hartford, State of Connecticut, 1916), 13.

Chapter Five

1. Twain, Mark. *A Tramp Abroad.* New York, Harper & Brothers, 1903.

Chapter Six

1. Thoreau, Henry David. "Walking," Atlantic Magazine, June 1862, Online. www.theatlantic.com).
2. Hazlitt, William. "On Going A Journey." First published in 'The New Monthly Magazine', 1822, as "Table Talk" No. 1.

Chapter Eight

1. Tolkien, J.R.R. *The Lord of the Rings.* New York: Harcourt Houghton Mifflin, 1974.

Chapter Thirteen

1. Teale, Edwin Way. *Circle of the Seasons: The Journal of a Naturalist's Year.* New York: Dodd, Mead, and Company, 1987.

Bibliography

Although I spent most of my time reading the Connecticut landscape, I am indebted to the following volumes for basic information about the state and its inhabitants.

Atlas of Connecticut Topographical Maps. State of Connecticut Department of Environmental Protection. DEP Bulletin 17A, 2000.

Barret, John J. ed. *Connecticut Walk Book.* 18th ed. The Connecticut Forest and Park Assocation, 1997.

Bell, Michael. *The Face of Connecticut: People, Geology, and the Land.* Hartford, CT: State Geological and Natural History Survey,1985.

Fuller, Tom. *Trout Streams of Southern New England.* 1st ed. Woodstock, VT: Backcountry Publications, 1999.

Garrigus, William H. and Iveagh Hunt Sterry. *They Found A Way: Connecticut's Restless People.* Brattleboro, VT: Stephen Daye Press, 1938.

Hardy, David, Gerry, and Sue. *50 Hikes in Connecticut.* 4th ed. Wood stock, VT: Backcountry Publications, 2000.

Shepard, Odell. *Connecticut Past and Present.* New York: Alfred A. Knopf, 1939.

Thoreau, Henry David. "Walking," Atlantic Magazine, June 1862, Online. www.theatlantic.com).

Turner, Alfred Milford. Report of the State Park Commission For the Two Fiscal Years Ending in 1916 (Hartford, State of Connecticut, 1916).

Wessels, Tom. *Reading the Forested Landscape: A Natural History of New England.* Woodstock, VT: The Countryman Press, 1997.

Workers of the Federal Writers' Project of the Works Progress Administration for the State of *Connecticut. Connecticut: A Guide to its Roads, Lore, and People.* Ed. by Odell Shepard. Boston: Houghton Mifflin Company, 1938.

Acknowledgments

Chapter Four, "Ancient Pathways," published in *Artistry of Life*, Issue 13, Summer 2007, "Past Lessons: Learning From History."

Chapter Eight, "Heart of the Giant," published in *Wilderness House Literary Review*, Volume 4, Issue 2.

Chapter Eleven, "Walking the Streams," published in *SNReview*, Winter 2007, Volume 8, Issue 4.

Chapter Seventeen, "Winds of October," published in the *Post Road Review*, October 2007.

HOMEBOUND
PUBLICATIONS

AT HOMEBOUND PUBLICATIONS WE RECOGNIZE THE IMPORTANCE of going home to gather from the stores of old wisdom to help nourish our lives in this modern era. We choose to lend voice to those individuals who endeavor to translate the old truths into new context and keep alive through the written word ways of life that are now endangered. Our titles introduce insights concerning mankind's present internal, social and ecological dilemmas.

It is our intention at Homebound Publications to revive contemplative storytelling. We publish full-length introspective works of: non-fiction, essay collections, epic verse, short story collections, journals, travel writing, and novels. In our fiction titles our intention is to introduce new perspectives that will directly aid mankind in the trials we face at present.

It is our belief that the stories humanity lives by give both context and perspective to our lives. Some older stories, while well-known to the generations, no longer resonate with the heart of the modern man nor do they address the present situation we face individually and as a global village. Homebound chooses titles that balance a reverence for the old sensibilities; while at the same time presenting new perspectives by which to live.

CPSIA information can be obtained at www.ICGtesting.com
Printed in the USA
LVOW10s0538290815

452042LV00003B/516/P